LIONS and TIGERS and TERRORISTS, Oh My!

How to Protect Your Child in a Time of Terror

PEBBLE CREEK
PRESSWORKS

Back cover photo by Idris + Tony - Courtesy of World of Wonder
About the Author photo by Lobeline Communications

Visit us at www.terrorism4kids.com

Dedication

This book is dedicated to families everywhere who want to live in peace and follow their dreams, despite living in a time of terror. It is meant to be shared between grownups and the children they love.

Author's Note

This book is intended to assist parents, teachers and the children they care about, in coping with the threat of terrorism. I have drawn on my own professional knowledge, training and experience in writing this book, and I have suggested various approaches based on traditional psychological principles. However, this book does not take the place of a personal consultation with an appropriate mental health professional. I encourage the reader to seek professional advice and appropriate counseling to deal with any specific problems your child may be having.

As I explain in the text, the story of Dorothy and the Wizard of Oz, first published in 1900 and now in the public domain, offers useful ideas that can help all of us understand and cope with our anxieties. The phrase "Lions and Tigers and Bears, Oh My!" – which originated in the classic 1939 film version – has entered our language as a light-hearted way of confronting our worst fears. I have borrowed these cultural artifacts for purposes of commentary and instruction, and my book is not affiliated with any of the copyright or trademark owners who have also made use of various elements of the story that L. Frank Baum first told n *The Wonderful Wizard of Oz*.

Acknowledgments

I would like to acknowledge and thank the following people for their special contributions to my expertise in psychiatry, children and terrorism:

Robert Cancro, M.D., Anna Freud National Centre for Children and Families, Harvey Kushner, Ph.D., Sharon Rohowsky, Ed.D., Mubin Shaikh, Henry Weinstein, M.D.

I would like to acknowledge and thank the following people for their support in the coming to fruition of this book:

Steve Carlis, Stephanie Conti, Brian Forbes, Maureen Forman, Jacquie Jordan, Ken Levine, Sylvia and Sidney Lieberman, Hank Norman, Tiffany Towers, Psy.D., Michael Wright

LIONS and TIGERS and TERRORISTS, Oh My!

How to Protect Your Child in a Time of Terror

THIS IS FOR YOU, PARENTS, TEACHERS and OTHER GROWNUPS WHO CARE FOR KIDS

In The Wizard of Oz, Dorothy and her dog, Toto, are swept up by a cyclone and transported to the Land of Oz. As she cautiously begins to explore, she cradles him closer and says, "Toto, I've a feeling we're not in Kansas anymore." This may be how you feel these days, as you try to make sense of the new world we live in, and figure out how you're going to gently explain 'terrorism' to your child without actually causing him or her to hide under the covers in 'terror'.

You can tell your child 'little white lies' about Santa Claus, or the Tooth Fairy, because those fun games are harmless enough, but grownups can no longer tell lies about terrorism, because there is nothing fun about it. And besides, kids find out the truth soon enough from the media, their friends, older siblings, and from overhearing you talk when you think they're not listening. Just the other day, when schools closed because of a terrorist bomb threat, many parents made up lies to try to protect their children from the ugly, scary truth. At least one mother told her little girl, "Schools are closed because it's too cold outside." And at least one father told his son, "Schools are closed because teachers want an extra day of vacation." But, when these kids went to school the next day, classmates – who had somehow heard the real story - told all the other kids the truth. So, now the children who had been lied to, are confused about words like "terrorism," and wonder why people called "terrorists" would want to bomb their school. Even worse, these children are confronted with the fact that their parents lied to them about something very important. You can try to explain that you only did it to protect them from the truth, but kids need to be able to trust you, especially when something scary is happening in the outside world.

Children need to know 'what's behind the curtain'. It's not a little bald headed man pretending to be the Wizard of Oz. It's an unfortunate reality about barbarians called terrorists. And the best way to protect children is to help them understand what terrorism is all about. Then, despite danger lurking in the shadows, they can become stronger and more resilient, in order to be able to follow their dreams. This is what this book will gently help you to do. First, read this part, meant for grownups. Then, you will be ready to share the next part with your child.

Age of Innocence

Underneath our 'super-cool adult' appearance, beats the heart of a child. Though society calls on us to be mature – especially now – in our heart of hearts, we secretly still want to believe that our wishes will come true when we blow out our birthday candles, and that we will live 'happily ever after', as the fairy tales promised. Even though we may be wonderful mothers or fathers, underneath we're nostalgic for our own childhood days, when we had parents who were responsible for taking care of us and keeping us safe. Suddenly, the innocent child in us has come face to face with uninvited evil, as our world is shattered by terrorist attacks. Whatever our chronological age, our 'age of innocence' has ended. If we feel robbed of our wishes and fairy tales, imagine how our children must feel.

It's a hard time to be a parent – and a hard time to be a kid. Besides having to feed, clothe, shelter and hug your children, you have to protect them from bullies, drugs, alcohol, shootings, pedophiles, gangs, copycat suicide... and now terrorism! What's happening in the world today can leave indelible impressions upon our little ones.

To be sure, even before 9/11, the age of innocence was already beginning to be soiled and shortened. Now, terrorism looms overhead, like black clouds out of place in children's crayon drawings. Raising happy, healthy children during these tumultuous times has suddenly become even more of a challenge - but not an impossibility. In fact, as you will read, our need to protect our children from terrorism may bring us unexpected rewards. When we commit ourselves to building stronger nests to keep our chicks safe, we build more loving families in the process.

The 'magic years' of childhood have long been under siege. Our grandparents or great-grandparents may have complained or boasted about having to trek long distances to school in the snow with holes in their shoes, or having to work long hours in factories or selling newspapers. But, later generations have been struggling with more psychological pressures than physical ones. Indeed, the sunny days of childhood were already troubled, before the wave of terrorist attacks, and the reasons for the troubles haven't disappeared.

Our children still face familiar fears, from the photos of missing children on flyers and freeway signs to the photos of murdered children on the news at dinner. Kids are already too aware of being counted upon to be self-reliant, when what they want is reassurance that they will be taken care of by their family.

But, gone are the TV-perfect families where the father is the breadwinner and knows best, the mom stays home baking cookies, and children get into harmless mischief that ends with laughter and hugs. Children, called upon at ever-younger ages to take care of themselves – and often their siblings – lack the practical and psychological resources to do so. The more chaotic the home environment, the less safe a child feels. Whatever problems exist in a family – marital conflicts, illness, financial hardship, addiction, and so on – the child often feels as though it is his fault. Youngsters feel pressured to live up to their parents' expectations.

School is stressful. Competition is fiercer than ever to get the best grades, wear the trendiest clothes and be in the in-crowd with the coolest kids. Schoolyards – even at the youngest levels – have become treacherous minefields strewn with bullies, drugs and sexual predators. Wholesome neighborhood playtime, crucial to developing socialization skills with peers, has been replaced by an isolating attachment to technology and social media. Children also 'comfort' themselves with unhealthy entertainment and junk food.

While yet in their cribs, many children begin a lifetime addiction to media violence: escalating from cartoons and action toys to more grownup entertainment. Research has indicated that the more media violence a child consumes, the more aggressive and desensitized to violence he becomes. He also tends to see the world as a meaner and scarier place. Now that terrorism has entered the picture, these children realize that the world is even meaner and scarier than they already imagined, and become overwhelmed.

So, even before the explosions of 9/11, the bloom was already off the rose of childhood. Our kids have had to struggle with thornier issues than their ancestors ever imagined. These troubles had already begun taking their toll, manifested as truancy, stress-related medical conditions, shoplifting, anxiety, depression, learning and attention deficit disorders, conduct disorders, alcohol and drug experimentation and a myriad of other problems.

Like most parents, you love your children and probably find these reflections hit too close to home. You want your sons and daughters to have a bigger, better life than yours, with more success, self-worth and security. Already feeling overwhelmed with the responsibility of putting food on the table and smiles on their faces, you've been grappling to get by, while barely keeping guilt at bay. Now terrorism is on the scene, as never before, and the precarious juggling act, called today's family, is tottering. Fortunately, help is at hand here.

Harry Potter, Superman, Supergirl and Batman to the Rescue

"I was hoping that Harry Potter would come," said a young girl, who had been held hostage in a terrorist attack on a school. "I was thinking he had a cloak that made him invisible, and he would come and wrap me in it, and we'd be invisible and we'd escape." Where is a good superhero when you need one? This is the question many children are asking themselves, as they invoke fantasies of superheroes coming to rescue them from terrorist 'villains'.

We know that terrorists have a history of targeting children. In 1995, for example, a plot was uncovered to release a chlorine gas bomb in Disneyland. In summer 2004, a computer disc, found in Iraq, contained photos, floor plans and other information about American schools in six states.

Child survivors of terrorist attacks remember the trauma. One year after one such attack, 7-year-old Chermen, recounted, "I was with my best friend, Oleg, inside the school. When the siege started, we tried to run together, but I lost him. Later on, I found one of the sleeves of his sweater. I never saw Oleg again. I found out that he had died.... I feel pain. And also rage. And since then, I want to avenge Oleg's death." Laima, a 9-year-old survivor, still draws pictures of terrorists, tears them up and sets them on fire – almost daily. "I draw the terrorists and burn them for all the children who died.... I want to take revenge on them for killing those children.... It's impossible to get enough revenge. All my life I will have to do it."

Are these simply fantasies of revenge that have not yet gone away or will these children grow up to hate and act out on their violent fantasies? It is understandable that children would want revenge for the devastation that terrorists leave behind, but it is a dangerous reaction – and not a solution. The most evil part of terrorism may well be the epidemic of hate, with which it can infect our children – unless we protect them.

We can't sit back and wait for Harry Potter to come to the rescue, although it seems increasingly apparent that, when J.K. Rowling wrote her series of books, evil Lord Voldemort (aka He-Who-Must-Not-Be-Named) had taken up terrorism and symbolized Osama bin Laden. The allegorical battle of Harry versus the elusive Voldemort (and his followers the Death Eaters – symbolizing Al Qaeda) paralleled our war against terror. Some characters feared that to 'name' Voldemort would acknowledge his existence, make him more powerful, or conjure him up. Similarly, today, some people fear that to acknowledge how terrorism has impacted our lives would be to conjure up our buried painful feelings. But, denial is neither rewarded in *Harry Potter*, nor in real life.

In a way, Harry Potter can come to the rescue, by providing you with a language in which you can talk to your children about terrorism. Dumbledore, the Head Master of Hogwarts School of Witchcraft and Wizardry, tells Harry, "You have a power that Voldemort has never had… you can love…. You are protected… by your ability to love." This is a lesson for children - not just wizards – to keep in mind.

For many kids, terrorism is so hard to wrap their head around that the only way they can comfort themselves is to imagine their favorite superhero swooping in to save them. This is especially tempting because Superman's Metropolis, Supergirl's National City, and Batman's Gotham City are easily compared to New York City, the site of 9/11. But, the more you help them understand what terrorism is all about, and all the 'real life superheroes' that are protecting them – from yourself to the police, firefighters, paramedics, National Guard, and so on – the less they will have to rely on imaginary superheroes.

Terror is Contagious: Infects Kids Around the World

A London student, Lauren-Amy, expressed her feelings in poetry after 9/11. "I wrote this poem, called 'Crash', because I couldn't get the events of America out of my head. I pretended I was a child in a Manhattan playground watching the tragedy unfold. I imagined what it would have been like and what I would have been feeling." Ironically, Lauren-Amy doesn't have to "pretend" or "imagine" anymore, since the events of 7/7 brought the "tragedy" closer to her home.

A bird is on fire
It's falling from the sky.
People jumping out of buildings
I really wonder why.

I walk along the playground
Until I see a plane
Stuck in the side of a building,
Now they're both aflame.
Along comes another jet,
Flying rather low.
I don't need to ask myself
Where it's going to go.

Smoke starts to fill the air
I look up in disbelief.
A building crumbles to the ground
I'm filled with shock and grief.

Sirens scream, people run
I don't know what to do
The dust and debris, thick like fog
Begin to block my view.

On the 11th of September
At 8.55 am
Began the slaughter of the thousands
Women, children, men.......

Confronting Our Own Feelings First

Are you in denial, pretending to yourself that 9/11, and the ongoing threat of terrorism, are not impacting your life? Or are you suffering from 'terrorism fatigue'? Or both? Whether you realize it or not, our family life, love life, work life, financial life, and all other aspects of our lives have been altered by this seemingly endless threat, leading some to adopt an unhealthy 'live for today' mentality.

We all wish we could protect children from an awareness of the horrors of terrorism, not just for a school day, but forever. Unfortunately, this is not possible, since even the youngest of them sense the impact of terrorism, as subtle as the tension in their parent's face, and we need to prepare our children to cope with potential future attacks. When you look into your child's eyes, as you broach the subject of terrorism, the choked up feeling you have is, in part, due to sadness for not being able to spare your child from the words you are about to say.

Do you know the biggest mistake that parents and other adults make when they communicate with children about terrorism? The biggest mistake is not acknowledging their own feelings. If you tell your children there's nothing to be frightened of, and that you, yourself are not at all frightened, your children will pick up on your fear anyway, and they will become even more frightened. This is because now the scary monster has become not only something out there, in the news, but inside their own home. You become the scary monster because you're not telling them the truth and they realize they can't trust you. This is a lot more threatening to them than terrorism. They'll feel confused, angry and betrayed.

When kids don't know what to believe, their imagination runs away with them, and stirs up scenarios that are far worse than the reality. This is especially true when they sense that the horror is beyond words, because you are not using words to describe your genuine reaction to it. Start by acknowledging your fears and whatever other feelings you're having. But then make it clear to them that, although it's always important to listen to the wisdom of one's feelings, you are not going to be stuck in them, and they don't need to be stuck either. You can tell your children what you plan to do to keep your family safe and to help other people during these hard times. Even more than what you tell them verbally, the most important message will be what you model for them in your behavior. If you admit that you are afraid, but then get on with life in spite of your fears, this will be a powerful lesson.

What you should never do is turn to your children for help coping with your feelings. Do not make them the parent and you the child. Too many children have been 'parentified' already, by overwhelmed parents who want help coping with the demands of everyday life. Regardless of how much you, too, may want to grab a teddy bear and hide from terrorism under the covers, you are still responsible for protecting your children. Your needs would overburden them, especially since they would blame themselves – not the terrorists - for your distress.

Before you can help your children endure terrorism, you need to be able to endure it yourself. It's the 'oxygen mask principle' of air travel. On airplanes, parents are instructed to secure the oxygen mask in place on their own nose and mouth before trying to secure a mask on their children. Why? It seems counter-intuitive, since you want to protect your children before yourself. But, if you succumb first, to the lack of life-sustaining oxygen, you will no longer be capable of helping your children. Similarly, you need to take steps to soothe yourself, before you can successfully comfort your kids.

The Birds and the Bees... and Terrorism?

When parents finally decide 'it's time' to talk about the birds and the bees, it's usually long overdue, since the little tykes have already been exposed to these topics through the television, their playmates, the Internet, and your overheard conversations. Similarly, by the time you brace yourself to talk about the awkward topic of terrorism, your children may well have their own – perhaps distorted – ideas.

So, before launching into a lecture on the finer points of terrorism, or what you think every child wants to know about terrorism, but is afraid to ask, you must first simply listen and observe them to determine how they are feeling.

Choosing the right time and place to talk about terrorism will depend upon many factors. Of course, you want to be sure that you have explained enough, so that they won't feel totally unprepared and helpless by the time another attack rocks their world. In order to provide your children with essential information, such as what they should do if they get separated from you or another responsible adult during an attack, you need to at least have had an introductory conversation about terrorism and terrorists. You can tailor the rhythm of your talks to their chronological age, emotional maturity, inquisitiveness, and what they already have seen, heard or experienced. Their need to know must be balanced by their need for calmness. It's important not to overwhelm them. Just as you can harm children by pretending that terrorism doesn't exist, you can harm them by forcing them to talk too much about it before they are ready.

Ideally, your children would come right out and ask you questions. Maybe they have asked some, but you were not paying attention. Perhaps their questions didn't include the word "terrorism," so you didn't understand that their tearful overreaction to a scraped knee or a tummy-ache was really a plea for you to soothe their fears about being injured in a terrorist attack. Or perhaps they asked one question, but have a zillion more stored inside their head.

If your children ask you questions about terrorism, answer honestly and simply, in words they can easily understand. It is best to answer in small bites of information sprinkled with reassurances that you are doing everything you can to keep them safe. They may choose an inconvenient moment to suddenly spring questions on you, as children are apt to do, such as when you are hurriedly dropping them off at school on your way to work. Or they may catch you off guard by their question, and without a good answer. Let them know that their questions are important and you want to respond to them with the care and attention they deserve. Then set a specific occasion, such as dinnertime, to discuss it with them. This way, they won't feel as though you are dodging their questions because it makes you uncomfortable.

If your children are not asking you questions, don't assume it's because they don't want to know, or because they know everything already. It is more likely that they don't want to upset you, or themselves, by talking about scary things. They may want to pretend that terrorist attacks never happened or that they will never happen again. It is also likely that they have been misinformed by their playmates, who have blown things out of proportion, as a result of their own fear or their desire to scare others, as they have been scared themselves. You can get your kids to open up by asking them what they know about terrorism and where they found out about it. Correct misinformation gently, so that they won't feel foolish or as if they need to defend their informant friends. Help children to understand the difference between rumors and facts.

Another reason why your kids may not be asking you questions is because they may be desensitized to real terrorist violence, because of having been steeped in media violence, or violence in their neighborhood. If they have had exposure to such violence, they may have already hardened their hearts and minds to it, as a way of trying to cope and not be swallowed up by the inhumanity. If your children are callous to the pain of others, you must address this immediately. Make sure that they understand the difference between real life suffering and make-believe. It is especially confusing for them to distinguish what is real on television, since both news and entertainment programming broadcast similar violent images. If they think terrorist violence is 'cool', then you must urgently put a stop to their exposure to violent images. This callousness is often a sign of serious psychopathology, for which psychiatric treatment is needed.

Do not misinterpret your youngster's silence or seeming lack of interest as their being unaffected by terrorism. Rather than feel relieved that they are not badgering you, note that these children may be quite traumatized but do not know how to express their feelings or don't feel safe doing so. Ask yourself if your own confusion or fear is causing you to give subtle messages to your children that perpetuate a cycle of silence. You need to let them know that you are receptive to talking about anything that's on their mind. You want to know how they are feeling and you promise not to get angry or laugh at them when they tell you. You're interested in what they think is going to happen. Unless your children are encouraged to come to you with all of their feelings, questions, worries and confusion, they will keep these things bottled up inside, until they leak out as psychological and physical problems.

You may not always be able to choose the ideal time and place to hold a talk about terrorism because you want to be responsive to their questions, which can pop out when you least expect them. And the time when you most expect them, amidst an attack or its immediate aftermath, is chaotic. But, if you're the one to bring up the subject, then choose a time when they are not distracted by some lesser disaster, such as getting a bad grade or having a fight with their best friend (which is not necessarily 'lesser' in their view of the world). An appropriate time is when they are feeling calm, good and comfortable, not when they are feeling tired, cranky or ill.

Bedtime is also not the ideal moment, nor is a child's bedroom the ideal place for you to initiate chats about terrorism. Whatever children think and feel before they go to sleep will be the stuff that dreams and nightmares are made of, if it doesn't keep them awake altogether. And wherever children are when you initiate these chats, may become a permanent storage place of these memories. So you don't want their room, their most private space, to become a constant reminder of their fears. But if they ask you a question, as you're tucking them in for the night, give them the reassurance they're really after, before they're left alone in the dark, and promise to give them a longer explanation the next day. Morning is a good time to ask them about their dreams. If they've had a scary nightmare, recounting it to you will help get rid of leftover jitters, as will drawing what the scary monsters looked like. In fact, the more they express the content of their nightmares, when they are awake, the less they will need to envision their fears when they are asleep.

It would be best to go to a natural setting, such as a garden, lake or beach. There should be little noise or disturbances, and no time pressure to be somewhere else. Having their favorite snacks along can be quite comforting. Your kids might want to set aside a certain time and place, such as dinnertime or Sunday walks in the park, as a 'safe zone' where they know you will devote yourself to answering all their questions – not just about terrorism, but about life.

Just because you've answered a question once, doesn't mean it will last them forever. Children need to hear answers over and over again, especially when it concerns something as confusing and emotionally disturbing as terrorism. They will be flooded by feelings, which will start to drown out your words. They may not remember ever having heard you explain it before. And if they do remember, they may want to hear it again, especially the parts that reassured them the most. At other times, children will let you know if you are giving them too much information at once. Their eyes may glaze over, they may suddenly find their toys a lot more interesting than you, or they may claim to need a drink of water or a trip to the bathroom while you are in mid-sentence. Save the rest for another day.

It is impossible to know the answer to all of your kids' questions, since the future is unpredictable. Don't make up sugar-coated answers off the top of your head, simply to reassure them. If you don't know the answer, all you need to do is promise them that you will look into it. Then you can make it a family project and go to the library or look on the Internet to show them what you've found. Though no one can predict the future, this will be good role modeling and will allow your child to feel some sense of mastery over terrorism.

If your children are of widely divergent ages, you will need to talk with them individually, as well as together. A general one-size-fits-all approach could be too overwhelming for the younger ones and unsatisfying for the older ones whose questions would run deeper.

If your kids are too little for verbal communication, you can 'talk' about terrorism by means of drawings, clay figures, toys, role playing and so on. Studies done within months after 9/11, indicated that children as young as 2 1/2 had learned to connect airplanes with crashing into buildings, even though their parents thought that they had had no exposure to the tragedy.

Babies, totally dependent upon their parents or parental figures, are unable to follow instructions, as to what to do in the event of a terrorist attack. The only questions they are likely to ask you are with their eyes, when you look frightened, depressed, angry or upset, or if they experience disturbing events in person or in the media. Even before babies say their first word, they can read faces and feel empathy. The best way you can talk to them about terrorism is through the hugs and kisses that will make them feel safe. In fact, no child is too old for reassuring hugs and kisses. It's a language all kids understand.

It would be so much easier to talk to children about the evil in the world, if we could reassure them there was no need to worry because the danger was far away, not on their doorstep. The concept of how far terrorism is from them is complicated by their awareness that it is actually in their living room or bedroom... inside the television. And young children believe that the danger can come out of the TV and get them. TV 'talks' to your children, too, in emotional and sensationalized language, burning terrifying images into their head.

Know that children will be especially intrigued by news that features other children, such as Martin Richard, the 8-year-old boy killed in the Boston Marathon bombing. It is especially tragic for them to see news coverage of children clapping after terrorist attacks have caused destruction. It is important to explain that these children have been taught to hate. They simply believe what their misguided parents or leaders tell them about us being their 'enemies'. As if they were cheering for the home team, they are excited and happy that their so-called enemies have been killed and injured.

No matter how your children react to learning about terrorism – and their reactions will be as individual as they are – their feelings must be respected, understood and validated as authentic. They mustn't be shamed or judged or told to 'get over it'. They must be allowed to cry, get angry, cling or sulk, at least for a while. Telling your child, "Don't cry. It will all be okay," stifles his emotions. And if your child senses that you don't really believe it will be okay, then he will be more confused and frustrated than before.

Parents are tempted to coax their children out of their murky thoughts and bad moods, because these unrehearsed, uninhibited reactions jolt parents awake from their denial and complacency. Resist any such temptations to soothe them with false or unrealistic promises. But you can let them know how much hope and faith you have that things really will turn out okay.

Suicide Bombers and Other Bullies

The number one question children will wonder about is, "What's a terrorist?" Though your youngsters may never have heard of Osama bin Laden, nor know exactly what ISIS or a terrorist is, they surely know what a bully is, if they are old enough to go out and play or go to school. Each day, countless children fear being attacked or intimidated by bullies whose cruelty and aggression is on the rise. In fact, many students skip school in order to avoid being a victim of the social jungle, where bullies, gossips, clique ringleaders and other predators roam.

You have an opportunity to bully-proof your child at the same time that you talk to them about terrorists, by defusing the mystique that makes such bullies loom larger than they actually are.

Children can best conceptualize terrorist gang members if you liken them to the big bully on the playground who teases and threatens kids and sometimes physically hurts them. Terrorists and playground bullies try to prove that they are more powerful by dominating, intimidating, and controlling their victims in order to get their toys and get their way.

Explain how the playground bully is bad to other children because he feels bad about himself — so he takes his frustrations out on them. The bully is actually jealous of them because he thinks that they have a happier life than he does. The bully's focus is on taking his victims down with him, even if it means risking punishment or pain, like suicide bombers who sacrifice themselves. No matter what the bully's problem is, he needs to be stopped before he hurts more people — in schoolyards or our backyards.

Indeed, playground bullies and terrorists need to be taught conflict-resolution skills. Until then, tell your child that your country is working hard to stop terrorist bullies, just as you would help your child stop any bully who might try to terrorize him. The way to rebalance the power between a bully and his victim is for the victim to build up strength — not just muscles, but also self-esteem. For, in order to prevent the bully from callously overpowering the targeted victim, the victim must stand up to the bully.

Out of the Mouths of Babes

Bombarded by the noise of news reports, playmates, siblings, and the din of overheard conversations at home, in school, on the bus, and in the street, children are easily baffled. They confuse "hijacker" with "kayaker" and ask themselves why kayakers would take over a plane. Or they confuse "Iraq" with "a rock" and ask themselves how a rock could cause so many problems. Or they worry that a four-legged wild animal is going to get them, when they hear about "lone wolf" attacks.

Here are examples of some more questions your children are pondering, whether or not they have found the courage to ask them aloud. These answers are simply one way to respond to such questions. You can use them as a starting point or to give you ideas that you can put into your own words. Your answers should reflect your personal values, philosophies, and religious or political beliefs. And remember, they should be tailored to the chronological age and psychological maturity of your children, as well as what they are emotionally ready to hear at any given moment.

Child: Will something bad happen to me?
Parent: I would love to be able to promise that nothing bad will ever happen to you. But I will always tell you the truth, so I cannot promise this. In a way, something bad has already happened to all of us, because we share the sadness of the families who have had loved ones killed or injured by the bad people, called terrorists. But we can learn so much from what happened. We can learn to appreciate things we didn't pay attention to before, like how much we love each other, how beautiful our city is, what wonderful friends we have and so many other things.

No matter what the specific question is that your children may or may not put words to, what they always want to know is how safe they are. So you should end your talks by reassuring them that many caring people are working hard to keep them safe. Give them examples of what is being done by you, your family, the government, teachers, doctors, nurses, firefighters, soldiers and other military personnel, airplane pilots and airport workers, police officers, the United Nations, and numerous others to protect them. Also, let them know that most people are good, most days there are no terrorist attacks, and even when one happens, most people are safe. So it is very unlikely that they or their family will be hurt in one. Although you cannot promise that there will be no more terrorist attacks or that nothing bad will happen to your children, you can promise that you will always love them, no matter what happens.

Child: Will something bad happen to Mom (or Dad) or my brothers or sisters?
Parent: I can't promise you that nothing bad will happen to me or the rest of the family, but I can promise that I will always do my best to keep you safe, just as I have always done. We are learning how to make our family safer than ever. We are taking the best care of ourselves, and each other, that we can. Looking out for each other and loving each other goes a long way towards keeping everyone in our family safe.

Child: Will I die? Will you die? Will my dog (cat) die?

Parent: What do you mean by "die"? What do you believe happens to people or pets when they die? What makes you believe this?

Before answering your children's questions about death and dying, it is important to find out what they already imagine. You may decide that there is no reason to challenge their beliefs at this time, if these seem to comfort them. Your answers will depend upon your personal or religious beliefs. Note that children, under age 7 or 8 or so, are not usually able to understand the permanency of death. Many parents would prefer to keep such questions shrouded in darkness, because it forces them to face their own mortality before answering. The more introspective and at peace you are with the end of life, the better you will be able to talk with your children about such touchy issues.

Child: What will happen to me if you don't come to pick me up at school or you don't come home? What if you get hurt?

Parent: You don't have to worry about being left alone to take care of yourself. If you are at school, the teachers will take care of you until someone from our family or one of our adult friends comes to pick you up. If I don't come home because I am hurt, then someone in our family or one of our adult friends will come home to take care of you. I will be in a doctor's office or in the hospital getting well. If you ever get scared because I am not where you think I am supposed to be, then ask a teacher, or your babysitter, or some other adult taking care of you, if you can call me. If you can't reach me, then call the people on the list of family and friends we made together. These people will take good care of you. You will always have someone to love you, no matter what happens.

Child: What is terrorism?

Parent: Terrorism is like 'bully-ism' - but it is a threatening plan to push people around carried out by adults — not playground bullies. The word 'terror-ism' comes from 'terror'. Terrorists are trying to make you feel 'terr-ified'. Imagine having to watch a whole lot of scary movies, one after the other. This is how scared they want you to feel. They are hoping you will be too terrified to go to school, play sports, have fun with your friends, go places with your family, or do anything else that makes you happy. They want you to be as miserable as they are.

Child: Is he (or she) a terrorist?

This will most likely be said loud enough for the person in question to hear, much to your distress and embarrassment. Your youngster will probably recognize — from news reports - some stereotypical physical feature (such as olive skin or facial hair) or traditional clothes (such as a man in a turban and loose turic, or a woman in a hijab or burka). Or they might just point to anyone carrying a backpack or who looks scary to them. Ask your child a question first.

Parent: What makes you think he (or she) is a terrorist?

Whatever the reason given, explain:

Parent: Not all people who look like that are terrorists and not all terrorists look like that. We shouldn't judge people simply by the way they look or dress, or by what country they come from or what religion they believe in. We can only judge people by what is in their heart. This is a free country. We can look or dress however we like. We can practice whatever religion we believe in. What we can't do is hurt other people by our words or our weapons.

We adults are told to be vigilant and to alert authorities if we are suspicious of a package or a person. Children can be taught, "If you see something, say something." But, making them paranoid or turning them into vigilantes would be damaging.

Child: What happened today (yesterday, last week) when we were attacked?

Your answer will, of course, vary according to circumstances. Keep it short and simple. For example:

Parent: Some bad people, called terrorists, went on some planes and crashed them. Or, some bad people, called terrorists, went into a building and shot the men and women who worked there. Or, some bad people called terrorists blew themselves up with bombs, which then hurt and killed some people in the nearby crowd. It was very sad. But there were a lot of brave firefighters who helped rescue people. And doctors and nurses are helping the hurt people get better. And the police are looking for the friends of the terrorists, to put them in jail to punish them for helping plan the attack.

Child: Why do terrorists attack us?

Parent: Terrorists want to hurt people who don't believe in the same things they do, like the same God they believe in. They want us to follow their rules. They don't want us to be free or to think freely with our own ideas. Terrorists are so full of hate that they don't know how to talk calmly with us about their feelings, their ideas, their religion and their reasons for being angry with us. So instead, they just have temper tantrums. Each time they explode a bomb, it is like they are having a big temper tantrum. You know that this isn't the right thing to do and it doesn't work. If you have a temper tantrum, you don't get your way, do you? Well, the terrorists are not going to get their way, either.

Child: Why do terrorists blow themselves up when they set off bombs?

Parent: Terrorists not only hate other people, who don't want to play by their rules, but they are full of hate for themselves. Terrorist leaders make phony promises to them. The leaders tell them that if they become "suicide bombers," by blowing themselves up when they blow up many other people, they will get rewarded when they die. Sometimes they also tell them they will make them into famous heroes forever or make their family very rich. The suicide bombers want to believe that these lies are true, because underneath, the hate and anger they have for themselves makes them want to destroy themselves. This is very sad for them and for us. If you ever feel that there are things you don't like about yourself or your life, I hope you will tell me what they are. We can make things better together. You should never hurt yourself or other people because you're angry.

Child: Will there be another attack?

Parent: There are a lot of people working very hard to make sure there is not going to be another attack. They are trying to find terrorists before they get close to being able to carry out any more damage. And they are punishing terrorists who have done bad things or who are plotting to do bad things. We hope this will stop other terrorists because they won't want to be punished, too. But, no one really knows if there will be another attack, or when or where. I can't promise that there won't be more. What I can promise is to get our family prepared, so that if there are any more attacks, we will be as safe as possible.

Child: What can we do to stop the attacks?

Parent: We can start trying to bring about world peace. It is not easy to make peace with terrorists because they are not willing to talk about peace or, if they do, they don't usually keep the promises they make. They find excuses to blame other people, so that they can keep being violent, instead. But, most of the people around the world do want peace, so we can talk together with them. Then we can all try to find ways to make terrorists realize how important peace is for everyone. Terrorists, who have done bad things in the past, may one day come to understand why they did these things and why they should never do them again. One of the ways to work towards peace is to try to teach people – like the terrorists – that they can choose to do good things from now on.

Politics 101

As citizens and politicians get increasingly fed up with terrorism, their political beliefs grow stronger and their voices louder. People become more polarized. Some support military action, while others are against it. Some are for laws to crack down on terrorists, while others are against them. Children are not as oblivious to these speeches or protests as you might think. They are often caught in the crossfire. Now it's not only the war on terror that they feel stressed by, but the 'war' between their countrymen, and perhaps even their family members, as to what actions to take. You need to make sure that your youngsters understand that just because family members, citizens or politicians disagree with each other's ideas, they are not likely to go to war with each other in a physically violent way – unlike the terrorists.

Whatever your political views, you should explain them to your children in a way they can understand. If you support military action, you need to give reasons why you think this is the best way to go. Be prepared to answer tough questions. Children may ask: "Why is it okay for us to kill people in Iraq, but not okay for terrorists to kill people in our country?" "When is it okay to kill?" "If you go away to fight, what will happen to me?" Though you may have good reasons for supporting military action at this time in history, be sure to convey the message that violence is not the ideal way to solve conflict, but may be a choice of last resort.

If you are against military action, you need to give reasons why you think this way, despite many of your country's leaders disagreeing with you. Explain how you can love your country and respect its leaders without agreeing with all their actions. Be prepared to answer tough questions, such as: "If we don't fight terrorists in other countries, won't they come here?" "How can we make peace with terrorists who don't want peace?"

These discussions provide opportunities to teach children, not only about differing political perspectives, but, about how the democratic process works, how to express opinions persuasively, and how to get along with people even if you disagree with them. Your youngsters will have friends who have opposing ideas to theirs. It is important to teach them how to have their views heard without putting down or losing their friends.

Minors and the Military

A child, whose daddy or mommy has joined the military and is stationed overseas, needs to be blanketed with special affection and love. Even when youngsters understand why their parents have chosen this path, and even when these youngsters are proud of how brave they are, they still may feel abandoned and wonder if their parent left because they were bad boys or girls. They feel angry about being abandoned, and then guilty about feeling angry. These children may react to the perceived abandonment by seeming to forget about their military parent, not talking about them and not wanting to correspond with them. It is their way of expressing displeasure and of withdrawing from the parent, so that they won't feel as sad if the parent dies.

According to Anna Freud, the founder of child psychoanalysis, "The experience of being left by a parent, for whatever reason, creates in children a whole host of conflicting emotions, on the one hand sorrow and longing, on the other hand despair, anger, and resentment. In some cases the negative feelings gain the upper hand and extinguish the affection. In others the opposite happens: love for the absent parent is increased beyond all measure, and the child remains tied to him."

Fortunately, there are ways to prevent negative feelings from gaining the upper hand. Children need to be reassured that they are not to blame for the seeming abandonment, that they will be well taken care of, and that their military parent misses them and still loves them very much. In fact, it is because of this love that their parent is willing to risk their life to protect their country for future generations. One appreciative little girl explained that her father's "job" in the military is "to keep us safe from those bad guys… so we don't get hurt or die."

Similarly, a youngster, whose older sibling has joined the military and is stationed overseas, needs reassurance that it is not the youngster's fault and that the sibling misses and still loves the child very much.

The family member, who is about to be deployed, should make an audio or video recording, leaving a 'living memory' for the child to play and replay while he is gone. He should remind the child of fun experiences they shared. He should tell him why he has chosen to join the military; how proud he is of the child for being a 'brave little soldier', too, for understanding his need to leave; what his hopes are for the child in his absence; and, most of all, how much he loves the child. A special possession of the family member should be given to the child for safekeeping, while he is overseas.

One little boy, whose father is in the military, pointed proudly to a photo and said, "This is a nice picture of me and my dad. It makes me comfortable because at night I pick it up and then I hug it, because I really like my dad."

Children should be encouraged to write, or send drawings and useful gifts, to their dad, mom or sibling, as frequently as possible. A 'buddy system', pairing one family up with at least one other family who has a loved one stationed overseas, will insure that children have friends who can relate to what they're going through.

Kids may not want to ask questions, or express their fears about the safety of their parent or sibling, in order to protect other loved ones. If they do ask whether their military family member will ever come home, promises should not be made to convince the child that he is certain to, or the child will never be able to trust again if he doesn't. It is better to admit that it is possible that he won't come home again, and that this is why it was so courageous of him to put his life on the line by joining the military. The child can be reassured by talk of how well his family member has been trained, what protective clothing he wears, and how the troops look out for each other.

In 6-year-old capital letters, one boy scribbled on the back of each envelope to his dad overseas, "BE BRAVE." The bravery of military personnel can serve as inspiration for all children. It can be explained that they are scared, too, sometimes, but they find courage in their heart to do what they believe in.

New Reasons for Nursery Rhymes

Themes relevant to the problems that children are struggling with today are reflected in vintage nursery rhymes. These can yet be reassuring to children. Such rhymes have a familiar lilting quality that is soothing. They convey the message that children of past eras had devastating events to endure, as well. But the principal psychological usefulness of these nursery rhymes comes from their being 'counter-phobic' in nature. That is, by turning scary situations into repetitive rhymes, that children can sing and play games to, they become less scary.

The story of the "Three Little Pigs" is especially useful for conveying the message of how important preparedness and resilience are. The Big Bad Wolf, like a terrorist, wants to destroy his prey. The first two pigs, singing, "Who's afraid of the big bad wolf?" are in denial, and don't take the threat seriously enough to prepare. Soon, the wolf is able to blow the house down of the first little pig, because it's only hastily made of straw. Then he blows the house down of the second little pig, because it's only carelessly made of sticks. But, he can't blow down the house of the third little pig because it's carefully made of bricks. The moral is that when you make the effort to build yourself up – psychologically and physically – like the third little pig did, you won't be as vulnerable to a terrorist.

The story ends with the third little pig taking in the first two, and together they set out a hot cauldron for the wolf to fall into when he climbs down the chimney. This teaches kids how important it is for us to help others, and how together we can fight terrorism.

"London Bridge is falling down… my fair lady." For centuries, children have sung this nursery rhyme, about the succession of disasters and restorations that this international landmark has undergone. Each time the bridge was destroyed, it was rebuilt more fortified than before: wood and clay, bricks and mortar, iron and steel, silver and gold, and finally, a man to watch all night.

The moral of "London Bridge" is that we should persevere against man-made and natural disasters, and use our ingenuity to strengthen our bridges and ourselves. It is just as relevant today.

How Will Our Children Reflect the Impact of Terrorism?

The savagery of terrorism is shattering and unfathomable to adults. Imagine how 'little' it makes children feel. These emotional experiences have deep effects on their still developing brains. They are witnessing too much, too soon. You know it's true, when you hold your child and feel his terror-stricken heart pounding poignantly in his chest. Early trauma causes children to feel painfully conflicted between a need to heal their world and a sense of helpless rage. The timeworn saying, "War is not healthy for children and other living things," continues to hold true.

Long after terrorist attacks occurred, a 10-year-old girl insisted she still smelled smoke at the site of the bomb explosion. A 7-year-old boy refused to ride the subway. A 5-year-old boy, riding his bicycle, panicked when he heard a low-flying plane, and ran inside. A 9-year-old girl insisted upon sleeping in her street-clothes, because she felt she had to be on alert at all times. An 11-year-old boy kept asking when another disaster would occur. A 4-year-old girl drew a picture of a bomb dropping on her home.

Kids may regress during times of stress like these. This means that they may go back in time, behaving as they did when they were much younger. They may start to soil their pants, or wet the bed again, or have nightmares and want to crawl into bed with Mommy and Daddy. They may whine or throw temper tantrums. They may be afraid of the dark or carry a favorite doll, toy or pillow around with them. They may suck their thumb. Don't become critical, impatient or angry with them. Don't shame them by calling them "babyish." Reassure them that it is a normal and temporary reaction to stress. These are signs that they need to receive more comfort from you. If these behaviors persist, you should seek professional advice.

Be on the lookout for other changes in your youngster's personality, behavior, thoughts or attitudes. It is the change itself that is significant. It means that his psychological balance has been disturbed.

Sometimes your children may seem to react inappropriately, such as by making jokes or exclaiming, "That's so cool!" when they watch a news report of a terrorist explosion. Be careful not to misinterpret their seemingly cavalier attitude as their not having deeper feelings, like fear, sadness or anger, underneath. They may be frightened of how bad it makes them feel or frightened of telling this to you. Ask your child if he really believes it's "no big deal," or if he's just trying to act brave because he thinks that's what's expected of him or because he doesn't want anyone to think he's a wimp. He may simply be copying the 'denial' behavior he has seen in you.

Unwittingly, parents are always influencing their kids. Studies found that children, aged two to six, who were asked to take their doll shopping to buy groceries for a party, were significantly more likely to buy cigarettes if their parents smoked, and to buy alcohol if their parents drank alcohol (or if the children watched PG-13 or R-rated movies). The implication is that your reaction to terrorism will be of paramount importance to your children, and will influence their reaction. They will 'buy' into your beliefs and behavior, whether it relates to cigarettes and alcohol as necessities for a party, or to courage and altruism as necessities for the fight against terror. Your children will sense your deepest feelings, and be confused by the mask of bravado you wear. Research shows that the intensity of children's symptoms of stress is proportional to the intensity of their parents' stress.

You may be surprised at how self-centered your children seem, when their concerns focus upon who will take care of them, who will keep them safe and who will love them. Understand that what might seem like narcissism or conceit is actually their survival mechanism, because young children can't take care of themselves. This 'healthy narcissism' is natural when they feel endangered. Once they feel their needs are being met, they are more able to think about helping others.

In fact, children's concern for others can manifest in their feeling survivor guilt, especially if someone they know has been a victim. Children can also feel guilty for having fun – when they think they're supposed to be somber all the time. A child might catch himself laughing, and quickly look around to see if anyone has noticed, just in case that would be considered naughty. Kids need to be reassured that they are not expected to carry the burdens of the world on their shoulders.

Children, who have already experienced traumatic life events, may have developed coping skills that then help them during the subsequent trauma of terrorism. But, for the most part, children who have suffered prior trauma will be more vulnerable to the impact of terrorism. For example, if a child has parents going through a divorce, has a physical illness, is anticipating a new sibling, or loses a close relative (not necessarily due to terrorism), he will already have a full plate before trying to cope with the threat of another terrorist attack. If a child has suffered traumatic events or losses, these memories may surface under threat of a terrorist attack. Similarly, if, on a background of a fresh threat of terrorism, a child then experiences an unrelated personal trauma, the psychological impact will be compounded.

Children, who already have psychological problems, will certainly be more vulnerable to the added burden of terrorism. If a child suffers from anxiety, depression, conduct problems or other mental health problems, he will be more at risk of these symptoms intensifying, and may even develop new ones. This is because his mind will process events through a lens colored by his pre-existing psychological problem and because he is already over-sensitive. These children should be in treatment with a mental health professional, if they are not already.

Additional factors that determine how vulnerable children are to the impact of terrorism, include: the temperament they were born with, their chronological and emotional age, the severity of terrorist attacks they have been exposed to, their physical proximity to terrorist attacks, whether their home or school has been damaged, whether they were in danger of being hurt or killed, whether they witnessed people screaming or being hurt or killed, whether they are displaced, whether there are economic ramifications, and whether they have a personal connection – such as a relative, friend, or friend of a friend - being hurt or killed in an attack.

In particular, exposure to media coverage makes children more vulnerable to the impact of terrorism. Studies, after 9/11, concluded that children who consumed more news about the event – via newspapers, radio, TV or the Internet - had more psychological problems, including anxiety, stress disorders, and depression. Each exposure to such news is a re-exposure to the event itself, which compounds the original trauma, and young children may believe that the event is actually recurring.

The more children believe that the world is a dangerous place, or blame themselves for the event, the more affected they will be. Children will also be more affected if they see their parent uncontrollably crying in front of them, have parents with mental health problems (including post-traumatic stress disorder), or live in the midst of family discord. But fortunately, the more supportive, harmonious and loving families are, the more protected children will be.

As much as we wish that our children would never have to feel any painful emotions, we can't and shouldn't try to prevent this when it is an appropriate reaction to life events. It is especially painful – for children and adults – to try to comprehend disasters caused by man's sinister acts against man. An important part of growing up is learning to recognize, understand and cope with their feelings. You can't make it all go away, but you can make them feel listened to and loved, no matter what their feelings are.

Some kids are able to get in touch with and express their feelings. Others are too overwhelmed to know how to begin. When your child cannot or will not talk about his feelings, his artwork can provide clues to them because it is normal for children to express their feelings about the world around them in their artwork. Dark colors or somber themes, such as black clouds, rain, violence, destruction or death reflect his feeling scared, sad, mad or bad. If he's scared, drawing the threat helps him feel some control over it. If he's sad, the black clouds in the drawing may mirror how he feels inside. Rain may symbolize his tears. If he's mad, he may scribble all over the drawing or rip it up after he's done, as a way of expressing his anger. And if he feels bad, his drawing will reflect his muddled malaise. But, if your child is preoccupied with expressing himself in dark colors and somber themes, it is likely that he is also showing other symptoms of his inner distress.

Research conducted after terrorist disasters indicate that parents underestimate the suffering of their children. So look carefully for signs that your children may be feeling scared, sad, mad or bad.

"I Feel Scared"

When was the last time you told anyone that you felt scared about anything?
Try it. It's remarkable how calm and relieved you start to feel, as the words are barely out of your mouth. Just the act of identifying or naming a fear helps it fade, as children intuitively understand. But, they also understand that admitting their fears puts them at risk of being ridiculed for being a wimp, and at risk for making the secret fear actually happen, once the secret is out.

It is normal for kids to be scared in the face of terrorism; not just of things directly connected to terrorism – like bombs and explosions – but of things that may easily be mistaken for a terrorist attack – like thunder and lightening. Fear is a self-protective reaction that we are all born with. During normal psychological development, children's fears, evoked by real external dangers, transform from one specific danger to another. Anxiety, not necessarily evoked by a specific external danger, is a more free-floating emotional state. Often fear and anxiety coexist. In some kids, normal fear and anxiety can escalate into a psychological disorder.

Here is a description of common fears of childhood, according to normal developmental stages. Fears can last beyond the stage in which they begin. And since terrorism can cause children to regress, it can also explain why your child may seem to exhibit fears belonging to a younger stage of development.

Infants (birth to 18 months) often have fears of loud sounds, bright lights, sudden movement, animals, objects and heights, as well as stranger anxiety and separation anxiety. Separation anxiety begins when the child becomes aware that loved ones exist even though they are out of sight.

Toddlers (18 to 36 months) may begin having bedtime fears. When kids can imagine what lurks in dark corners, they begin to fear the dark. They also fear wetting the bed and fear bedtime separation. Toddlers' separation anxiety results from inner conflict between wanting to cling to parents and wanting independence. They also have a fear of water, and disappearing down the drain or being flushed down the toilet. They are afraid of new situations and certain people (like doctors, who are associated with illness and pain).

Preschoolers (3 to 5 years old) may continue having bedtime fears, but now they center on nightmares, nighttime fantasies that children have difficulty distinguishing from reality, and night terrors (in which the child moves around in a type of trance). They also have fear of death, which to them means parental abandonment, since they don't yet understand the permanency of death.

School-age children (6 to 12 years old) may continue to have bedtime fears and separation anxiety, though they should gradually be conquering some of their fears from preceding stages. At this stage, fear of social disgrace - other kids making fun of them or not liking them - takes over. They fear not measuring up or failing, in school or on the playground. Their maturing comprehension of death causes them to worry about harm occurring to themselves, their loved ones or society. They may engage in risk-taking behavior to try to prove that they can conquer their fears. As they get closer to puberty, they worry more about being found attractive and popular.

'Magical thinking' is a normal part of child development. The child believes that his thoughts, words or actions will cause or prevent a specific outcome in some way. This is a mistaken belief, since it defies commonly understood laws of cause and effect, but it is real to the child. Children's magical thinking may include believing that they are responsible for terrorist attacks. For example, a child may believe that his not sharing a toy with a Muslim schoolmate caused an attack.

When fear or anxiety becomes excessive, it can manifest itself in behavior, such as whimpering, crying, screaming, rambling speech or becoming mute, hyperactivity or immobility, shyness, clinging, fidgeting, thumb-sucking, nail biting, leg shaking, voice trembling, or avoiding eye contact. And it can manifest itself in thought processes, such as worry.

As children's cognitive development matures, they start to make predictions about future events and anticipate misfortune, allowing them to worry in a more complex manner. They may worry, not only about their own safety, but about the safety of friends and loved ones. Children who worry excessively and uncontrollably, and tend to catastrophize situations, by focusing upon the worst possible outcomes, may develop a generalized anxiety disorder.

Separation anxiety has long been a commonplace reaction, occurring when children have to separate from home or from their parents, such as when they start school or play at the home of a new friend. Nowadays, even children who have already passed through this stage may again feel separation anxiety - especially right after a terrorist attack. Not only will children have the typical anxiety about their parents leaving and going somewhere unimaginable, where something bad will happen, today, they worry that their mom or dad's workplace, bus or train station will blow up, or their plane will be hijacked. They also worry about something bad happening to themselves in their parents' absence, or of never being reunited with their parents. Separation anxiety is symbolic of children's fear of loneliness, starvation, helplessness and destruction.

In anticipation of, or in response to, separation, children may cry, cling, shadow their parent, or complain of physical symptoms (especially stomachaches, headaches, nausea and vomiting). They may refuse to be left alone at school or at home. Since fear creeps in along with darkness, they may also refuse to be left alone in their bed. Kids, desperate to maintain a connection with a parent, plead for another story, glass of water, light or blanket. Once a parent leaves a child's bedroom, the child may crawl into the parent's bedroom and bed, or fall asleep outside the parent's door. Whatever children envision as a threat to their family, they express in nightmares, and in waking fears - of everything from monsters to explosions to airplanes falling from the sky.

Separation anxiety may be intensified if a child has 'lost' a parent through death or divorce, or through a parent's chronic physical or emotional illness, including alcoholism or other substance abuse. A hidden source of separation anxiety may stem from children discovering that their playmate's parent has joined the military and could be sent overseas. These children may be afraid to ask, but are wondering whether their parent will be next. Anticipate their questions, and let them know if it is true.

Since our modern world provides a more realistic basis to once irrational fears of parents disappearing because of 'something bad' happening to them, it is a little more difficult to determine what is normal separation anxiety and what is a separation anxiety disorder. If your child's separation anxiety interferes with school attendance, or with participating in activities and play-dates, then seek professional help.

Post-traumatic stress disorder in children is similar, in some ways, to the disorder in adults. There are the essential symptoms related to exposure to the traumatic event, intrusive thoughts of the event, avoiding reminders of the event, negative changes in thinking and mood, and changes in responsiveness (such as being more easily startled). But PTSD in children differs in other ways. For example, they may compulsively reenact the traumatic event by repetitive play that expresses themes or aspects of the trauma, without relieving anxiety. Their distressing dreams may transform, from specific dreams of the trauma, to generalized nightmares of monsters or less recognizable frightening content. In order to feel less helpless, they may develop 'omen formation', which is an unrealistic belief in their ability to foresee future traumatic events. Some of the triggers or reminders of the trauma that they try to avoid may not be obvious at first. For example, a child who was eating strawberry jam on toast, on the morning of 9/11, may never want to eat it again.

Since terrorism is not simply one traumatic event that ends, but is rather an ongoing threat, it strains the definition of PTSD, which typically describes a child or adult who continues in survival mode, even though the threat is no longer present. PTSD is known to actually cause chemical, metabolic and structural changes in the brain that can affect coping behavior. If you suspect your child may have post-traumatic stress disorder, consult a mental health professional.

Anxiety may manifest itself as an obsessive-compulsive behavior. A common example is the "step on a crack, break your mother's back" rhyme that children chant, as they try to avoid cracks in the sidewalk. Just as with other anxiety disorders, terrorism feeds some symptoms. For example, if children have heard about bio-terrorism, their concern about germs and contamination may not be as irrational as it once would have seemed. Yet, if your child becomes obsessed with cleanliness or decontamination rituals, when there is no real threat, it's a sign that their anxiety is out of control. We must be careful not to allow children's fears to overwhelm them, such that symptoms become chronic and disruptive of their life. If this begins to occur, seek professional advice.

Children's anxiety about terrorism can also take the form of a phobia (particularly agoraphobia, the fear of crowds or public places) or panic disorder. These reactions are more disruptive to a child's everyday life than normal developmental fears, and require professional consultation.

"I Feel Sad"

A third-grader in the U.S. expressed sadness by drawing the twin towers, and next to them, a heart broken in two. Children all over the globe feel the effects of terrorist attacks no matter where they occur. Alex, a London student, expressed sadness in a poem, entitled "The View."

Waking this morning
What do I see?
No twin towers
Looking at me

People emerging
Out from the rubble
Choking and crying
So much trouble

How can so few people
Take so many lives
A young woman falls
Another person dies

I'm really really sad
To see a great building go
So many people buried
Down, down below

Waking this morning
What do I see?
No twin towers
Looking at me

Sadness is a normal reaction to terrorist violence. In fact, if your child isn't feeling sad, you should be concerned. Let them know it's okay to cry. It doesn't mean they're a baby or a coward. In fact, a good cry is a wonderful way to release all the sadness that's been building up inside. Show approval when your kids are being empathic with the sad feelings of others who lost loved ones, or who were hurt. But, be aware that sadness can become more severe, evolving into clinical depression.

Depression in children is similar to adult depression, but there are some differences. Depressed children are frequently sad and tearful, but sometimes a child's sadness may be expressed as an irritable or cranky mood. You may feel that nothing seems to please your child, who is losing interest in activities, isolating himself from his peers, spending a lot of time alone, withdrawn and seeming bored. A depressed child usually has sleep disturbances, trouble falling or staying asleep, or sleeping too much. Similarly, there is often a disturbance in eating too much or too little, and gaining or losing weight. He may complain of physical symptoms, such as stomachaches or headaches. Declining school grades may reflect poor concentration, low energy or frequent absences. A depressed child is extremely sensitive to rejection or failure. Depressed children may feel worthless, hopeless and sure no one could ever love them. They may talk about, or actually make efforts to, run away from home. If your youngster talks about giving away his favorite things, or leaves a list lying around designating who his things should be given to, it is a cry for help. It signifies that he expects to die – either due to outside danger (like a terrorist attack) or due to inside danger – his sad feelings.

There is now the added risk of some kids wanting to be like suicide bombers, and, consciously or unconsciously, making real suicide attempts. This copycat suicide behavior could be a result of the youngster not appreciating the dangerousness of his self-destructive act, or a result of depression. It can be an attempt to get as much attention as a suicide bomber, or an attempt to terrify others because of how terrified the child feels. If you notice one or more of these symptoms, bring your child to a mental health professional, since even young children can commit self-destructive acts.

"I Feel Mad"

Kids find it easier to say, "I feel mad," when what they really feel is "hurt" or "scared." Adults do this, too. It is a way to save face. We don't want to let others know how vulnerable we are when someone hurts our feelings or something scares us. Pay attention to what your child really means underneath his words. If you feel that he is truly mad, then know that it is normal for your children to feel mad about the senseless violence that terrorists perpetrate.

Children express their anger most often towards the people they feel closest to, usually their parents and siblings. They are testing you, to see if you will still love them, even when they are angry.

They may also express anger towards specific ethnic groups or communities, whom they fear as dangerous invaders. It is not unusual for kids to have revenge fantasies, which they delight in describing. Such behavior allows them to pretend to be braver than they feel inside. Revenge fantasies can help your children cope with their feelings of helplessness, and can be part of the healing process, as long as they know not to act upon their fantasies.

But, you should not stir up your youngster's anger by talking furiously about seeking revenge and retaliation. Terrorists and their fellow gang members should be punished, and it is understandable that we would want to hurt them for hurting us. But we don't want to stoop to being as irrationally blinded by hate as terrorists are. Your children will be frightened if they feel your vengefulness is out of control, or if they misinterpret your anger and feel that you are blaming them for terrorists' acts.

Teachers on duty in playgrounds note that after terrorist attacks, the schoolchildren play games, pretending to blow themselves up. One interpretation is that they are internalizing the anger that they feel towards the terrorists, by directing it inward and 'destroying' themselves. Another interpretation is that they are identifying with the aggressor. By pretending to be terrorists, they are aligning themselves with the power that terrorists have been exerting over them. This gives them a sense of mastery, so that they feel less intimidated and more powerful themselves.

Children who are born with an aggressive temperament, or who have suffered abuse at the hands of a parental figure, sibling or bully, are more likely to have their inherent aggression kindled by the flames of terrorism. Similarly, children who have difficulty expressing their feelings about terrorism verbally, may, out of frustration, resort to physical expression.

Aggressive children risk hurting themselves as well as others. They must be evaluated by a mental health professional, to determine the origin of their aggression, since it will only grow as they grow up, unless it is treated.

"I Fee Bad"

When children can't or don't distinguish between feeling scared, sad, mad or other emotions, they may just experience themselves as feeling bad. They feel blurred emotions, vague discomfort, uneasiness, or malaise. It is very important to help your children understand the different meanings or uses of the word "bad." There are the 'bad' feelings of uneasiness your child may experience. There are your child's 'bad' or naughty behaviors. And then there are the 'bad' actions of terrorists. You do not want your child to think that you are saying he is as 'bad' as a terrorist.

Kids feel confused. They may mix up unfamiliar words and unfamiliar people, places and events. The younger they are, the more they will have a 'cartoon view' of the world. If buildings, airplanes or people fall down, or if buses or train stations blow up, they expect them to reboot themselves again in a flash, just as they have watched them do in cartoons. It is hard for them to understand what is real and permanent and what is make-believe.

One London boy told his teachers that close relatives, including some children, had been killed in the 7/7 bombings. The teachers were suspicious, as there were no reports of child casualties. They spoke to his mother, and she confirmed that he was making it up. What would make a child do such a thing? One possibility is that adults, unaware of how bad he was feeling, were fussing over the news and neglecting him. He wanted someone to pay attention. Another possibility is that he wanted reassurance from his teachers that his relatives were actually safe. Yet another possibility is that he was suffering from post-traumatic stress disorder, or another psychiatric disorder, that distorted his reality; in which case, he should get professional help.

Some children withdraw from the environment and life experiences, as a way to protect themselves and avoid being vulnerable in a world that now seems more dangerous. They may shun emotional risks, like close friendships, or physical risks, like contact sports. Ask them why they have stopped participating in the world the way they used to enjoy, and gently ease them back into life with a lot of encouragement and support.

Other kids, stressed by terrorism, may be more prone to accidents, such as falling off their skateboard or bicycle. This may be caused by carelessness, recklessness, an unconscious wish to hurt themselves, or inner turmoil causing them to be distracted. While some risk-taking behavior can be a normal part of growing up and testing boundaries, a preoccupation with defying danger is a symptom of an underlying problem that should be evaluated by a professional.

How to Raise Happy, Healthy Children in a Time of Terror

An unexpected benefit of terrorism is that it makes us more attentive to the psychological needs of our children. In the past, when terrorism seemed like something that happened only to other people, we may have been lost in the demands of our everyday life. But, today, we look more closely at how our children are coping with their world. And the key to helping children cope with terrorism is to lovingly fulfill their needs as they pass through each of the developmental phases of childhood. This will build resilience to all of life's challenges – not just those due to the impact of terrorism.

Here are 88 ideas for things you can do right now to make sure your children are happy and healthy:

1--- Help your children get in touch with their <u>feelings</u> and get comfortable with expressing them to you. For very young children, this may mean your drawing or making at least four faces, to correspond with the basic feelings that terrorism can instill in them. Label the faces: scared, sad, mad and bad, and have your child point to how he's feeling today. You can also draw or make other faces, such as happy, confused, brave and so on. Body language – using the whole body – conveys the feeling even better. So try adding the rest of the body to your drawings or when you act out the feeling. Older children can draw or make their own faces or can tell you in words how they're feeling. You can suggest that they draw two self-portraits, one showing how they look on the outside and one showing how they look on the inside. The very act of expressing their feelings gives children a sense of mastery over them.

2--- <u>Empathize</u> with your child. That is, put yourself in their shoes and imagine what it must feel like to be them.

3--- Encourage your children to ask you <u>questions about terrorism</u>, terrorists and terrorist attacks. Encourage them to also ask about things that terrorism has made them think of, like: death, ambulances, the human body, weapons, religion, politics, war and peace. Let them know that no question is off limits.

4--- Spend <u>quality and quantity time</u> with your children. Make sure that every day includes time that you devote to each of your children exclusively, to make them feel special, loved and protected. If possible, set aside a particular time every day for each of them, so that they can count on it. Don't let yourself be pulled away by telephone calls, texts, or other distractions. Stay focused on your child during their time. This is the best buffer against the stress of terrorism, and the best way to build self-esteem.

5--- Plan <u>family fun time</u> – at least one special event every week. Take turns selecting what you will do, so that each family member feels important and gratified. For example, the family could play games together, take a long walk to a restaurant for dinner, go to a concert, or stay in for a 'movie night'. More important than the activity itself, is the togetherness.

6--- Give each of your children a special <u>token of your love</u> to carry with them at all times, as a reminder that your love is always with them. This could be a heart necklace or ring, a small stuffed animal, a photograph, or something else that holds special meaning for you both. It will help your child to feel protected by your love.

7--- Carry a <u>photo of your kids</u> with you at all times. Let them know that you are keeping them close, in a locket or wallet. And keep a photo of the whole family on your desk at work and somewhere special at home. Though your children may not acknowledge how much it means to them, they will be thrilled to know how much you treasure them.

8--- Be aware of your own vulnerability to becoming transfixed by media coverage of terrorism. It can, not surprisingly, be as <u>addictive</u> as other media violence. The psychological impact this will have on you will make you less able to meet your children's needs.

9--- <u>Do not allow children, younger than school age, to watch TV</u>. You may set them down in front of a seemingly innocuous program, and it can suddenly be interrupted by news reports about terrorists. Or they can change the channel and inadvertently come upon news about terrorist attacks or other violence. Even these glimpses of terrorism will confuse and upset them. If you are at home with them and want to watch a kid-friendly show, they can be in the room with you. But, it is better to have them watch children's videos or DVDs instead, so that you can control what is being fed into their minds.

10--- <u>School age children should only be allowed to watch TV in bite-sized pieces,</u> and only when you're watching with them, to explain things and to stop them from biting off more than they can chew. Studies have shown that children want adults to protect them from scary news. All television viewing should be limited. Sparingly, kids may watch news reports about terrorism, but only if there is a beneficial purpose to it – not just curiosity or morbid fascination. One purpose would be to reassure them that they are being protected, such as if the news tells of terrorists being brought to justice or of first responders helping the injured. Another purpose would be as a means of getting your children to open up about terrorism. Television can gather us together under an electric blanket, if families watch it mindfully. Be sure to physically comfort them, by hugging or holding hands while you watch. When you shut off the news, ask your kids how it made them feel.

11--- No child (of any age) should have a television in his or her bedroom. They can - and will - turn it on, when you are not around to supervise what they are watching. The replayed images of destruction – although terrifying – are also mesmerizing.

12--- Similarly, you need to manage your child's access to the Internet, so that they don't come across disturbing images of terrorism while they are searching for answers to their homework or playing computer games.

13--- It is best not to listen to the news on your car radio while you are driving your children to school. Though they may pretend to be nonchalant when they're in the car with you, they will be distracted all day in school by the scary news they heard, instead of paying attention to the teacher. It is better to play audiotapes or CDs of soft music in the car and talk to your children about their day. If you need to keep track of an unfolding dangerous situation and must listen to the news for updates, be sure to turn the radio off quickly as soon as you have heard what you need and talk to your children about what was in the news. At home, for brief updates, you can listen to the radio with headphones.

14--- It may be difficult to prevent kids from seeing, at least the front page of, newspapers when they are outside the home. Make sure they feel comfortable coming to you with their reactions to the headlines and anything else they may have read.

15--- Involve children in disaster preparedness, so they will not only be informed as to what the family's plans are, but also empowered to carry out these plans. For example, you can: go together as a family to buy supplies for your emergency kits, decide upon who to call and where to meet if you get separated, assemble a list of important family information for your children to carry with them. You can have each of your kids choose a favorite toy to include with the sleeping bags and other evacuation supplies. Explain that, if it is necessary to leave home for a safer place, it will be like going on a camping trip and there will be other families there, too.

16--- Make sure that there are always <u>art</u> supplies available: crayons, paints, charcoals, clay, building blocks, pipe cleaners and so on. Inspire your children to use them often. Feelings and questions about terrorism, that they may not even be conscious of, will come out in their artwork. Expressing themselves in this way will relieve some of their tension. Ask them gently to tell you about their work. Though some of their darker themes may disturb you, do not tell them to draw happy suns instead. This will convey the message that they can't show you their dark feelings and will make them push these feelings down even further, where they will do greater damage.

17--- Recognize the value of getting into the habit of having <u>open dialogues</u> with your kids. Once they feel comfortable coming to you with their feelings about terrorism, they'll open up about their other everyday stresses – such as how they feel about being picked last for a team or not being invited to a birthday party. Maintaining open dialogues is the key to helping children deal with stress.

18--- <u>Sleep problems</u> can be a source of tremendous frustration for children and their parents. Try to set a consistent bedtime routine, including soothing rituals such as milk and cookies, storybook reading and hugs and kisses. You can also give him a special huggable toy or blanket to sleep with, as a 'transitional object' to hold onto and remind him of your love. Night-lights and a flashlight under the pillow help dispel fears of the dark. Keeping a cassette or CD of lullabies, gentle music or favorite songs in a player on his nightstand, will help comfort your child.
Some nights this will not be enough. If, for example, your child is feeling particularly anxious after a bad day, or if he has a nightmare, it may be necessary to stay with him in his bed until he falls asleep. You may let him sleep in your bed, as long as you are careful not to let this seem like a reward for his anxiety or nightmares, such that it becomes a persistent unshakable habit. Although at times it may seem tempting to let your child crawl in bed with you, out of convenience, or to soothe your own fears or to avoid having intimate relations with your partner, this is not a healthy pattern to get into. If your child has regressed to an earlier stage of development, he may need to return to bedtime diapers for a while, and should never be punished for accidents. Punishment would only increase his anxiety, regression and consequent bedwetting or other toilet accidents.

19--- <u>Read books together</u>. Read biographies of courageous people, such as Helen Keller, Martin Luther King, Jr., Anne Frank, Stephen Hawking or Malala Yousafzai. Read fiction books to allow your kids to identify with the people, animals or fantasy characters, especially those who are learning to overcome challenges. It is less threatening for them to talk about these characters' feelings than their own. Stories are a wonderful way to get children to open up about personal issues.

20--- Suggest that your children express themselves in <u>writing</u>. Poems, diaries, stories or essays are excellent ways to help them figure out for themselves what they're feeling about what is happening around them. Some children feel less threatened if they can put their thoughts together in writing before talking to you about them.

21--- Encourage your children to write <u>letters</u>. They can send their opinions to newspaper editors; their sympathy to families who lost loved ones; their gratitude to the troops, police or other first responders; and their recommendations to political leaders. If they are too young to write, then they can send their message in drawings.

22--- Recommend that your children <u>draw pictures of – or make lists describing - situations</u> when they feel scared, sad, mad, and bad, and when they feel the opposite: brave, happy, loving and good or calm. Whenever they are feeling one of the unpleasant emotions, have them consult the list and do what makes them feel the opposite. For example, if they are feeling scared because their school is closed for the day due to a bomb scare, you can take them to visit a fire station, where the firefighters will let them look at the fire engines and help them to feel brave. Then they can add this to their list or draw pictures of these opposite experiences.

23--- <u>Parents often expect boys to be tougher</u> than girls, not only in muscle, but in reaction to upsetting events. Yet studies indicate that boys start out a lot more sensitive than people realize. It is only after around the age of 4, that boys become less willing to share their feelings after sensing that others want them to "act like a man." Stifling boys can cause them to become emotionally isolated for the rest of their life.

24--- During those moments when your children do not feel like talking to you about terrorism, you might suggest that they talk to their stuffed animals or pets, until they are ready to share their feelings with you.

25--- Nurture the capacity for empathy that your kids are born with by fostering their ability to imagine what it feels like to be in another person's shoes. You can turn this into a game, by asking them what they think everyday people are feeling. You can play this game anywhere - from storybooks to supermarkets.

26--- Use a globe to show children where events are occurring in the world. It will reassure them to know that many of the dangerous places and sites of terrorist attacks that they hear about in the news are far away from where they live.

27--- Use more localized maps to show children where events are occurring in your city and your country. Though some terrorist attacks may not be as far away as you and your children would like, it is still reassuring for them to know exactly where these frightening events are taking place, because it gives them a small sense of control or mastery.

28--- Demonstrate patriotism. Teach your children more about your country, to nurture their appreciation of it. Encourage them to display the flag, read national authors and sing along with patriotic music.

29--- Take your children to museums-especially the 9/11 Memorial Museum and 9/11 Tribute Museum-and art galleries. Not only is this a valuable education in itself, it will provide the family with new ways to approach talking about terrorism. Children may look at an abstract painting and ask whether you see the face of a terrorist in it. Or they may look at an exhibit of ruins of an ancient civilization, and ask whether, one day, children will be looking at an exhibit of ruins of their country's civilization. Answer their questions and then point out the beautiful artwork and other inspirational accomplishments that people have created throughout the ages.

30--- Take your children to the underline theater. These fantasies are wonderful escapes for children's imagination, which have been working overtime to try to make sense of their scary world. Afterwards, you can talk about some of the characters and themes, and what lessons can be learned. The happy endings of children's theater will reassure your kids that most stories, like lives, turn out well after all.

31--- Engage your child in playing with puppets. They can be store bought or handmade, even made out of paper bags. Children love to put words in their puppet's mouth. When kids pretend that it is the puppet's words, rather than their own, it gives them the freedom to express their true feelings.

32--- Utilize music to help your children get in touch with their feelings and to soothe them. Listen to music at home and take them to classical concerts or those created especially for kids. Encourage them to learn to play a musical instrument, a wonderful way of expressing their feelings.

33--- Get your children involved in physical activities, including: team sports, individual sports, dancing, gymnastics, yoga, running, walking or even playing with a ball in the backyard. These are effective ways for children to burn off tension and release stress-reducing hormones. In addition, team sports teach children cooperation, an important skill in conflict resolution. Horseback riding teaches children to face their fears and 'jump' over them. Incorporate physical activity into family fun time, such as by flying kites, raking leaves or building a snowman or sandcastle together. Physical activity builds children's self-esteem, at the same time it builds healthy bodies and brainpower, making them feel more confident in their abilities to survive terrorism.

34--- Just like adults need social support, so do kids. Make sure you arrange plenty of play-dates, so that your children can confide in each other about their fears and other feelings, while having fun, too.

35--- Plan get-togethers with extended family, as frequently as possible, to enhance your children's sense of being surrounded by an extra security blanket. Tell stories of how your relatives of today, and those from long ago, proved their resilience by surviving traumatic events in the past – such as world wars.

36--- Involve your children in wholesome activities, like <u>Boy Scouts and Girl Scouts</u>. Consider becoming a troop leader, to contribute to the enrichment of kids' lives and to make your kid proud.

37--- Make sure your home is not all gloom and doom. Filling it with <u>laughter</u> is an antidote to feeling 'scared, sad, mad and bad'. To supplement your own sense of humor, you can read joke books together, or watch funny TV shows or movies.

38--- Respect your youngster's <u>individuality</u>. Don't push him to be like you or like his siblings in his reaction to terrorism.

39--- Don't be misled by kids' <u>overreactions to physical complaints</u>. If you simply focus on putting a band-aid on his bruised elbow or serving tea and honey for her tummy-ache, you may be missing the deeper psychological wound that they want you to soothe. Some children may not be able to put their emotional hurt into words, and direct you to a physical one instead. Other children may not want to admit that they have an emotional wound that needs soothing.

40--- <u>Praise</u> each of your kids at least once a day. They will know if you are not being sincere, so be sure to find something that they say or do that you can applaud. Tell them they are brilliant, beautiful or clever, or that you are proud of them, or that their viewpoint is an interesting way of looking at some matter. The more self-confident they feel, the more successful they will be in school and the more resilient they will be in life.

41--- Building self-esteem starts from the moment a child is born. A baby develops a sense of his worth when he sees the faces of his parents looking back at him. Parents' faces are like mirrors for a child. If parents believe that their baby is a marvelous treasure, their eyes will reflect that back to the baby – and the baby will 'know' that about himself and feel good. Make sure that you <u>mirror positive attributes</u> and feelings to your children, throughout their life.

42--- Help your children to regain a sense of having some control over their life by allowing them to be a part of <u>decisions</u> about everyday matters, such as what they will wear, what they will eat, or where the family will go for a weekend outing. Otherwise, they may attempt to take control in inappropriate ways.

43--- Help them to gain a sense of competency or self-confidence by allowing them to take responsibility for, or to assist you with, <u>family chores</u>, such as setting the table, washing clothes or gardening.

44--- You can help your children feel more secure by always being <u>trustworthy</u>, so that they won't doubt whether you will keep your promises – such as when you promise to return to pick them up at a certain time. Never sneak out without saying good-bye, since such trickery will crush a child's trust in you.

45--- <u>Don't model fearful or avoidant behavior</u>, and don't communicate that they cannot handle age-appropriate challenges on their own. You need to help them distinguish between situations that are truly dangerous and those that are simply challenges to overcome.

46--- Incorporate the <u>family photo album </u>into your life – and make it a habit. Looking at the pictures will provide a sense of history and continuity, and remind your kids of the many fun experiences the family has shared. Together, add new photos to the album regularly, to convey the expectation that there will be many more fun experiences in the future.

47--- Making <u>future-oriented lists</u> is also a good way to replace foreboding thoughts with hopeful ones. Kids can plan everything, from their day to what they want to do when they grow up.

48--- Model and teach good <u>problem-solving skills</u>, to help your kids overcome problems, one step at a time. You don't have to have all the answers, but you can demonstrate an eagerness to find out what you need to know and to think things through. Play games together that foster problem-solving skills.

49--- Teach your children <u>safety rules</u> for all frightening situations they are likely to encounter, not just terrorism. For example, make sure they are aware of 'stranger dangers', and how to say "no" and run if a stranger offers them candy or a ride.

50--- When any family members <u>travel</u>, be sure to let your kids know about the precautions that have been put in place to protect passengers, such as more thorough passport and baggage checks, bomb-sniffing dogs, and heightened terminal security. If the kids are not traveling with you, be sure to call them when you get to your destination to reassure them that you are safe – and thinking of them. Postpone trips that will take you away from your children, if they are going through a particularly difficult time.

51--- Turn your tots into globe-trotters. This is a great way to promote a better understanding of other cultures and an appreciation for their treasures. There is nothing like a family adventure in another country to foster closeness, mutual reliance and trust, which will remain when you return, and have to confront 'adventure' on your own turf.

52--- Keep in close communication with the schools your children attend. Find out what is being taught about terrorism and what emergency plans the schools have in case of attack.

53--- Tell teachers about anything you've noticed in your children that may impact their behavior in school, such as trouble sleeping which may make them drowsy, or anger which may make them act out. They are unable to learn until they feel safe and secure. So keep in close touch with teachers and school counselors to try to improve your child's sense of security, behavior and grades.

54--- Let teachers know about questions your children are asking, which they may be able to answer in more depth, such as about the history of terrorism. But, do not rely upon school to communicate your personal values, religious beliefs, philosophy of life or other opinions. You should communicate such thoughts yourself.

55--- Sometimes, kids' school behavior and performance can give a false impression of their not being as emotionally affected by terrorism as they actually feel inside. Their competitiveness, fear of failure, or the structured school routine, can help them to hold it together, at least for a while. But, if your child's school performance is faltering, arrange for a tutor to help get him back on track. Poor grades damage self-esteem.

56--- When a terrorist attack occurs, it is natural for you to want to rush to your child's school and take them home with you right away. In some circumstances, this may be a reasonable course of action. But, before you charge in, ask yourself whether you are doing this more for your own comfort or because you believe it is safer for the child. If other children have not been told of the attack yet, you may well start a panic. If you need to see your child, to make sure he or she is safe, call and let the administration know that you would like to come in and <u>help around the school</u> to reassure yourself. If you and your child feel good about it, consider volunteering on a more regular basis.

57--- Find <u>volunteer opportunities for your child</u>. Kids can't combat terrorists. But they can overcome their feelings of helplessness by volunteering to help those less fortunate than themselves, such as poor or disabled children. They can visit the elderly, bring food to the homeless, or help out at animal shelters. They can also accompany and assist you whenever you volunteer. Kids, who know that their parents are doing something positive, will feel more hopeful and optimistic.

58--- Kids can also '<u>volunteer' at home</u>, by going out of their way to surprise people they care about. For example, kids can clean up their room without being nagged, sort through their old toys and find some to donate to other children, or make a card to cheer up a friend or relative.

59--- Get behind your children's <u>fundraising</u> efforts to help those affected by terrorism. These can include: bake sales, lemonade stands, going door-to-door for donations, selling their drawings, doing chores for your family or your neighbors, and so on. They can collect money for the victims of terrorism, families of injured first responders, or a similar charity of their choosing. They can also collect items, like food or clothing, for people in need.

60--- Keep your child's daily and weekly <u>routine</u> as predictable as possible. Unfortunately, many families' routines have become unpredictable because they depend upon parents' workloads. But, it is important to make an effort to keep to scheduled mealtimes, play time, homework time, bath time, family time, bedtime, school and after-school activity time. The more consistent and predictable a child's routine is, the more life seems as though it's back to 'normal'. It allows them to feel in control of their personal world, and be better able to deal with the unpredictability of the next attack.

61--- Post a master calendar of each family member's schedule somewhere in your home that is easily accessible to children, such as on the refrigerator. This will make the future seem more predictable.

62--- Every morning, let your children know where you will be, during the parts of the day when you will be separated from each other, and how they can reach you there. Write down your approximate schedule, including the times, places and phone numbers.

63--- Consider buying your kids a cell phone. It will be comforting for them to know that they can talk to you if they're feeling scared and that they can reach you in an emergency. And it will be comforting for you to know that you can reach them, or even locate them if their phone has a global-positioning system (GPS). As many family members as possible should carry cell phones.

64--- Teach children simple strategies they can do on their own to quickly address their uncomfortable feelings. For example, when they're feeling scared, they can calm their breathing and visualize the place they feel the safest. When they're feeling sad, they can think about happy memories and positive plans. When they're feeling mad, they can count to 10.

65--- Make sure your children's play doesn't get out of hand, stimulated as they are by world events. Set limits and intervene if it becomes too rough, hurtful or scary. When kids think that their parents have stopped setting limits or their behavior, they feel as if the parents don't care about them anymore. And kids will keep testing the limits, in an effort to reassure themselves that their parents are still keeping a watchful eye on them.

66--- Helping children cope with terrorism is challenging. Along with all your efforts to take care of your kids, don't forget about yourself. Take some 'me time' to relax, do your favorite things, replenish yourself and surround yourself with support of your own. This is especially important if you are a single parent, and do not have supportive backup at home.

67--- Parents who you meet at school, at after-school activities, or in the community, are struggling with some of the same questions you are, and would be happy to share their stories and solutions. Why not set up a weekly or monthly 'parents' night' and meet in each other's homes? Or why not plan play-dates where you and the other parents chat while the kids are playing?

68--- If you need more intensive support, in order to be able to provide calmer and more responsive parenting to your children during these times, seek professional help for yourself.

69--- Be aware that anyone who abuses alcohol or drugs is making themselves, and those they care about, more vulnerable to terrorists. Not only are they emotionally unavailable to build resilience in their children, but, they're incapable of good judgment during an emergency situation.

70--- If possible, consider simplifying your life, such that your family could live on less income. Either one parent could stop working to stay home with the children, or both parents could cut down on the number of hours they work, in order to be with them. If this is not possible then, at least, rearrange your work schedule, so that one parent can be with them when they're not in school. Nothing will reassure children more than having their parent, literally, 'there' for them.

71--- Do not turn your children into latchkey kids. This was not appropriate before terrorism, and is surely not appropriate now, when it is a lot more dangerous and frightening for them to be home alone. Arrange for your children to be somewhere where they are supervised and preferably able to continue to learn and have fun. This could be after-school activity programs, sports, tutoring, the library, a babysitter, a grandparent, or a friend's home where there is a parent.

72--- Do not punish your children in a harsh or physically abusive way. If your kids are straining your patience and you're feeling short-tempered during these stressful times, remind yourself that spanking is a form of physical abuse, and choose a gentler form of punishment, if punishment is warranted. Teach children 'a lesson', literally, not physically. Always explain to a child what he did wrong and how he can do it right the next time. Harsh, critical or demeaning words, especially if they are shouted in a thunderous voice, constitute emotional abuse. The scars it leaves on a child's psyche are as painfully real and indelible, as scars from physical abuse. Often, it is punishment enough when a child sees how disappointed you are in him.

73--- <u>Listen to yourself.</u> Do not talk about things – on the telephone or in person – that would frighten your children if they overheard you. Children pick up on hushed or worried tones of voice, as well as content. It is also scary for them to see adults huddled together talking about something, or watching something, that they are trying to keep from the children.

74--- <u>Anniversaries</u> of significant terrorist attacks, such as 9/11, may trigger children's emotions, such that regressive behavior and other symptoms may intensify or appear again. Let them know that theirs is a normal reaction to being reminded of this shattering event. Prepare your children for news reports, so that they don't think that a new attack is occurring. Ask them how they would like to commemorate and honor the victims and the heroes. Your family might want to participate in a community remembrance ceremony. Or you might want to plan your own simple ceremony at home, such as by planting flowers, or lighting a candle and saying a few words or prayers. Talk to your children about what has been accomplished during the past year to make them safer, and what they can do to make the world a safer and better place in the future.

75--- Starting when they are very young, involve your children in your family's <u>religion</u>. With its traditions, beliefs, and ancestral history, religion can be quite comforting to children living in these uncertain times. It allows them to feel that God or a Higher Power is watching over them and keeping them out of danger, especially if you pray with them. Take them regularly to services at your house of worship. Read scriptures or other classic texts, as well as folk stories which have been passed down from one generation to another. Enroll them in religious school classes and special children's services. Celebrate the holidays and practice other traditions of your religion at home. Teach them prayers and encourage them to find their own voice when praying. If you are an atheist or agnostic, explain the reasons for this. Perhaps terrorism, itself, has weakened your belief in a God or Higher Power. The universe is not always understandable. Tell your children what religion their ancestors practiced and allow them to learn about this religion and to attend services to see if it is meaningful for them. Be aware that children can starve from spiritual malnutrition, if some form of spirituality is not offered to them.

76--- Learn about other religions, as well as your own. In particular, your children may well be curious about the Islamic religion and what goes on in mosques.

77--- Do not permit 'Muslim-bashing' or condone Islamophobia. If you discover that your child has been name-calling, teasing, or in any other way mistreating a Muslim, Middle Eastern person or anyone else from a different ethnic background than himself, find out why. Does your child have a reason to dislike a particular person, or does he believe his prejudice is justified, or even encouraged, by news reports of terrorism? Your child may not even know what the hurtful stereotypical words mean that he is using to discriminate against this other person. Explain that your child's words and behavior are painful. Model, by your own words and behavior, that you are not prejudiced.

78--- Teach tolerance. Explain that most Muslims, believers in Islam, are not terrorists or 'bad guys'. They want to live peaceful lives, too. Inform your youngsters about how some Muslims are cooperating with your country's leaders to root out terrorists, and contributing to society in other ways. If they have Muslim classmates, remind your children that these classmates are just kids – and that terrorism is not their fault. Arrange for them to play together or to collaborate on some project for school or the community, so that they learn to cooperate and depend upon each other.

79--- Help your youngsters to distinguish between tolerance, on the one hand, and submission or over-indulgence, on the other. Muslims find pigs offensive. But, other children should not be deprived of extraordinary literature, like _Winnie the Pooh_ (because of Piglet), or fairy tales, like _The Three Little Pigs,_ or pig toys. Such stories and playthings were not created with the intent to offend any particular culture or religion. Political correctness can be taken too far.

80--- After you have explained your political perspectives, and your children have had a chance to ask questions and make up their own mind about issues such as whether they support military action or laws to crack down on terrorists, get them involved in the political process. Depending upon their age and passion for activism, you can help them to: draw pictures or write letters to politicians, participate in protests or peace marches, attend speeches, or join a like-minded group working to influence decisions.

81--- Invite a child to dinner, whose dad, mom or older sibling is in the military. This teaches your child how important it is to show gratitude to people who are helping to keep their country safe.

82--- Give lessons in love of mankind. Describe how adult terrorists were not born that way. Unfortunately, they were taught as children to hate. Emphasize the importance of loving our fellow man, as we are all human and life is fragile.

83--- Children care about what happens to people in other countries, too, especially the children in those countries. You can support their compassion by teaching them about the United Nations and helping them to raise money for UNICEF to help children all over the world.

84--- Just say "No!" to violent entertainment. Just as you carefully monitor whether junk food or healthy nutrients go into your child's stomach – it is at least as important to monitor what is fed into their mind. If commercials, that last mere seconds, sell everything from soap to cereal, then it's not hard to understand how media, that glamorize violence, can sell murder and mayhem. Terrorism feeds on messages being spread all over the globe by violent media that teach people killing is fun, cool and exhilarating. Replace your children's violent media with more positive and inspirational entertainment. Explain the rationale for this philosophy in a positive manner, so that your kids don't feel like they're being punished. Once they understand that you are doing this because you love them, they will come to appreciate your rules.

85--- Discard all of your children's war toys, including toy guns or other weapons, action figures and camouflage outfits. It is one thing for them to use their imagination to bite their sandwich into the shape of a gun, and quite another for them to have an arsenal in their closet. When parents feel powerless, they unconsciously want to protect their children by 'arming' them. The threat of terrorism makes us more vulnerable to the allure of toy guns, action figures and camouflage clothes – especially when we see them 'advertised' in news reports. Some children act out imaginary scenes of terrorism to try to cope with the real scenes they've watched on TV. But you should not provide the props. Put up a sign that says, "This is a war toy-free zone" or "This is a peace zone." Substitute positive 'props' related to terrorism, such as a doctor's kit, a toy ambulance or fire truck, and other educational toys. Empower them from the inside.

86--- Parents talk to their children more about war than about peace, according to research. Teach your children that <u>peace</u> is the ultimate solution to the world's problems. Together, learn as much as you can about how to bring peace about. Read biographies about peacemakers like the Dalai Lama or Gandhi. Practice conflict resolution and anger management. Role-play more harmonious solutions to problems. Demonstrate how to peacefully resolve arguments in the home. Then help them resolve arguments with their friends and classmates. Talk about ways that characters, in TV shows or movies, could have resolved their conflicts better; and ways that political leaders and other newsmakers can resolve their conflicts better. Play songs like John Lennon's "Imagine" and "Give Peace a Chance." Ask your child's school to include 'peace education' in the curriculum. Join peace-making efforts.

87--- Don't let terrorism take over their childhood. Try to stuff their days with as much good old-fashioned <u>innocence</u> as possible, so that they run with joy, not fear.

88--- Tell your children "<u>I love you,</u>" at least once a day. An "I love you" a day, keeps terrorism fears at bay!

When Do Children Need Professional Help?

As you take this advice to heart, by talking to your kids about terrorism, recognizing changes in their feelings and behavior, and responding with action to help them cope, you now have the best chance of defusing their budding problems. Families are the first line of defense when it comes to protecting kids from the psychological impact of terrorism, and nurturing their resilience. But for some children, it may not be enough.

Kids who are struggling to cope may try to pretend they're okay, in order to protect their parents from having to worry about them, especially if they feel that their parents are having too many problems of their own. But, it is extremely important that you don't go along with your children's bravado, by pretending that no danger exists, or by pretending that they really are okay, when they're not. Be aware that your own distress may make it more difficult for you to recognize your children's signs of distress.

Kids may also try to pretend they're okay, in order to avoid talking to a mental health professional about the feelings that terrorism brings up, because it will remind them of the very issues they are trying to deny. But this is a necessary part of getting better.

Perhaps you've been thinking that your youngster is feeling or behaving in a way that is just a normal phase of childhood, or just an understandable reaction to terrorism, or just going through a stage that will pass. Now you realize that his feeling scared, sad, mad or bad can already be, or can become, a symptom of something more serious. Scared can translate into an anxiety disorder. Sad can translate into depression. Mad, may be a sign of a behavioral disorder, and can erupt into violence, directed outward towards others or inward towards themselves. And bad is a murky condition that should be explored, in order to know what it would translate into, before it does.

Terrorism can cause psychological trauma, creating emotional memories of distressful events, and storing these memories deep within the brain. If whatever is bothering your child, is not getting significantly better despite your efforts to fix the problem, or if it interferes with his life - school, activities, friendships, family, or physical health – then it's time to seek professional help.

Certainly, any child who has been directly affected by terrorism, such as by having lost a friend or loved one, by witnessing an attack, or by being physically injured himself, needs professional help. If you suspect that your child may be self-destructive, get assistance immediately.

Mental health professionals can help your child to sort out his feelings and to understand what is causing his psychological problems. These professionals will also help you to understand your child better, so that the whole family can heal. Treatment may include: individual psychotherapy, family therapy, group therapy, a support group, play therapy, guided imagery, cognitive behavioral therapy (CBT), art therapy, grief therapy, relaxation therapy, anger management, crisis counseling, EMDR (eye movement desensitization and reprocessing), and sometimes psychiatric medication.

Now that you understand how to protect your child in a time of terror with security blankets of love and affection, you're ready to put this knowledge into action

There's No Place Like Home

At the end of The Wizard of Oz, when Dorothy is safe at home once again, she hugs Toto with glee and says, "There's no place like home. There's no place like home. There's no place like home...!" Now, you are ready to create this same feeling of snug comfort for your child. Start by sharing the second part of this book with them, in mini-bite-sized portions. You can decide how much you want to read together at one sitting, depending upon the age and emotional maturity of your child. How you share this book with them will also depend upon such factors as: what you think they may have already heard about terrorism, what misinformation you need to correct, and whether there are any other stressors in your family at the moment. Be sure to create a calming, comfortable atmosphere each time – with pillows, their favorite stuffed animal or toy, their favorite snack, and anything else that makes your child feel cozy – as you help them explore their thoughts and feelings.

LIONS and TIGERS and TERRORISTS, OH MY!

THIS IS FOR YOU, KIDS

Do you know the story of The Wizard of Oz? In this story, Dorothy, the Tin Man and the Scarecrow start off together to find the wonderful Wizard. They skip merrily along, until night comes, and they find themselves in a strange forest. Dorothy turns to her friends and says, "I don't like this forest. It's dark and creepy. Do you suppose we'll meet any wild animals?" The Tin Man answers, "We might... mostly lions and tigers and bears." Dorothy and the Scarecrow shiver in fear. They never expected to come across wild animals on their journey. "Lions? And tigers?" they ask, hoping it's not true. But, the Tin Man nods his head and says, "And bears." They can hardly believe it. As they continue bravely – and a little more carefully - down the yellow brick road, they sing together, "Lions and tigers and bears, Oh my!"

These days, you don't have to worry much about lions, and tigers, and bears, because the ones you see are mostly in the zoo.

But, you may be worrying about terrorists, right?

You've probably seen news reports about terrorists on TV or the Internet, or heard about them on the radio.

You may have heard your mom and dad talking about terrorists when they thought you were asleep. Or maybe you heard your teachers whispering together in the hall.

Some grownups rush to turn off the TV or radio when news reports of terrorism come on, or catch you looking up terrorism on the Internet and get upset. Or, they suddenly stop talking about it when they see that you're listening.

They are only trying to protect you from becoming afraid of some bad things that are happening in the world. Adults wish that these things weren't happening, and they are hoping that these bad things will stop before you ever have to find out about them.

But, you already have seen and heard more than these grownups realize. Your friends at school tell you stories about what they think terrorists do, and it sounds like the scariest horror movie you've ever watched. You're not sure whether to believe them. It's very confusing, because you don't understand exactly what is happening or why.

It makes it scarier if grownups won't talk to you about it. It's especially frightening when you can see that your mom or dad are really worried, even though they pretend that there's nothing to be worried about.

You wish your mom, dad, teachers, and other adults you trust would simply tell you the truth. Then, you could decide what you think and how you feel. That's why they're sharing this book with you. It will help you understand this thing called 'terrorism', and learn what you can do to feel safe.

WHAT IS A TERRORIST?

What is a terrorist?

A terrorist is like a big bully on the playground......

Terrorists try to make us 'terrified', which means they try to make us so afraid that we stop doing the things we like to do and hide under the covers. For example, they want you to stop going to school, stop having fun with your friends at movies or concerts, and stop playing sports or taking ballet lessons. Terrorists want your parents to stop going to work and stop shopping. They want families to stop traveling on trains, buses and airplanes. They want to take over our wonderful country and our way of life because they are jealous of it, and they want us to follow their rules instead.

Draw a picture of what you imagine a terrorist looks like.

What makes you think a terrorist looks like this? Do you think all terrorists look like this? How else might they look?

Terrorists are called many names, like ISIS, ISIL, Al Qaeda, Daesh or lone wolves. But, whatever fancy names they like to call themselves, terrorists are simply 'bad guys' and 'evil-doers' who use threats and violent surprise attacks to try to bully people, so that they can be in charge. Terrorists can come in all colors, shapes and sizes. What matters is what is in their hearts.

Osama Bin Laden is the most famous terrorist. As the leader of the terrorist group called Al Qaeda, he plotted the terrorist attacks on America of September 11, 2001. To punish him and prevent him from plotting more attacks, he was killed by the American military.

Why are terrorists trying to hurt people?

Some terrorists are called "radical Islamists" or "radical Muslims." This means that they are not like most Muslims, who are peaceful.

Troubled terrorists are misinterpreting the Muslim holy book, called the "Koran," in a way that gives them an excuse to kill.

These terrorists say that they are making a holy war to please their God, who they call "Allah," by hurting people who don't believe in him. But, there is nothing 'holy' about hurting people. They call this war "jihad." Jihad means "struggle." Terrorists claim that they are supposed to struggle violently against their enemies, the people who don't believe in their religion. But, terrorists are really struggling with problems inside of themselves that make them angry. And they take this anger out on other people. They believe in lies that tell them they will be rewarded in heaven for killing "non-believers." Most of these terrorists live in faraway countries in the Middle East, where they even hurt other Muslims.

There are also "domestic terrorists," people who were born or raised in the United States and who are angry that they weren't able to reach the American dream of a perfect life. So, they want to hurt people who are successful and happy. Domestic terrorists feel lost and alone, so the terrorists who reach out to them on the Internet, from faraway countries, or in their neighborhoods, can more easily convince them to join their gang of terrorists, and become famous by causing a terrorist attack.

Although some terrorists may become famous for a little while, most are killed by their own bombs or by the police who protect us. Or, they are put in jail for a very long time.

What is a terrorist attack?

When terrorists make things explode and go 'boom', it's like they're having a gigantic temper tantrum. They sometimes use guns, knives, bombs, and even airplanes, to attack people. They especially like to target places that are symbols of the American or Western way of life, and where they can try to hurt a lot of people. The first terrorist attack on American land is called 9/11. On September 11, 2001, terrorists took over two airplanes and crashed them into the Twin Towers of the World Trade Center in New York City, because they were the tallest buildings in the world, and many people, who do important work for the United States, had offices there.

That same day, the terrorists also crashed planes into the Pentagon, the offices of the United States Department of Defense, near Washington, D.C. But, on a plane that may have been heading to the White House, brave passengers fought the terrorists and stopped the plane from reaching their target. All of the terrorists on these planes were killed when the planes crashed.

BREAKING NEWS
TWO PLANES CRASH INTO TOWERS
OF WORLD TRADE CENTER

Since then, a terrorist who we call the "Shoe Bomber," went on an airplane with a bomb hidden in his shoe. And a terrorist we call the "Underwear Bomber," went on a plane hiding a bomb in his underwear. Can you imagine hiding a bomb in your underwear? It sounds pretty silly, but this is how troubled and evil these terrorists are. They are even willing to blow themselves up in order to hurt other people. Terrorists who kill themselves when they are attacking others are called "suicide bombers." The "Shoe Bomber" and "Underwear Bomber" weren't able to blow up the planes, after all, and they are now in prison for life.

Now when we go to the airport, everyone has to pass through security checkpoints. Have you ever had to walk through a metal detector or watch your parents take off their shoes? This is to protect us by making sure there are no terrorists on the plane who are hiding anything that could hurt us.

The next big attack on America was called the Boston Marathon bombing. Two brothers came to the United States from a country near Russia. Though they went to school in America, the older brother felt like he never fit in, never had friends, and had many disappointments that made him want revenge. He convinced his younger brother to help him put bombs at the finish line of the race. The older brother was killed during the attack and the younger brother was put on trial and will never get out of prison. There have also been attacks on some other places in the U.S., like a nightclub in Orlando, Florida.

Terrorists don't just target America. They target all countries where people are free to follow their dreams. For example, an attack in London, England, that's called 7/7, hurt people on trains and buses.

In Paris, France, terrorists got angry at a magazine because it had a cartoon in it that they didn't like. They didn't want anyone to be free to draw or write anything that was against terrorist beliefs, so they went to the office of the magazine and shot the people who worked there. How awful is that? Killing people over a cartoon!

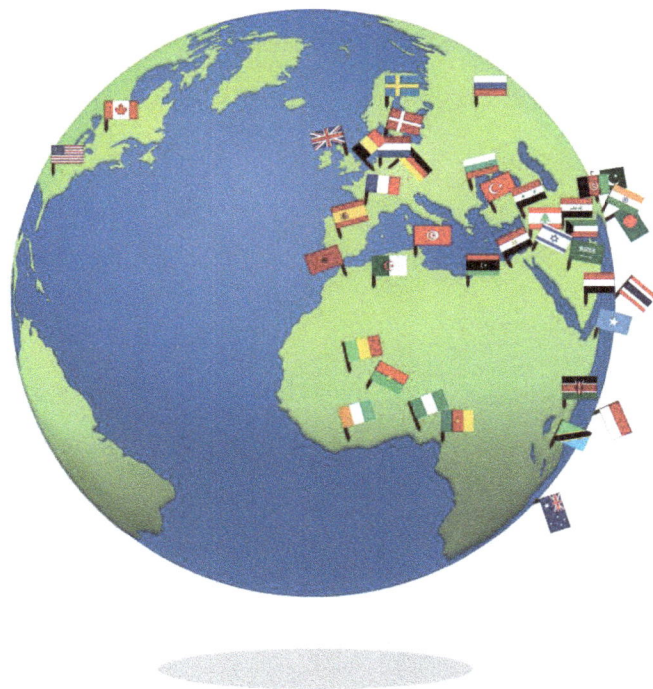

You may have also heard about attacks in Belgium, Spain, Israel, Africa and other places.

Why shouldn't you be scared of a terrorist attack happening to you?

There is more chance of you getting run over in the street, if you don't always look both ways, than being hurt in a terrorist attack. There are many other everyday accidents that are more likely to happen than terrorist attacks – like falling off your bicycle or skateboard, or getting hit in the head with a basketball.

Besides, there are people working every single day to protect you from an attack. For example, it's the job of the mayor of your city, the governor of your state, the President of the United States and Congress to protect you.

You may have heard of the F.B.I. (Federal Bureau of Investigation) and Homeland Security. These are big organizations with really smart people who work around the clock to find out who the terrorists are and what they are plotting, so that they can stop these plots to attack us before terrorists can make them happen.

There are also "first responders," who are ready all the time to rush to your aid if there ever was a terrorist attack. These first responders include police officers, firefighters and paramedics with ambulances.

Your mom and dad and teacher will protect you, too. They are reading the first part of this book, the part that's for grownups. And they are learning more ways to help you stay safe.

HOW DO YOU FEEL?

It's very important for you to dig down deep inside and ask yourself how you are feeling about terrorists and the bad things that they do. If you name all of your feelings, you can have more control over them. Here are some ways for you to find out just how you are feeling.

Draw a picture of yourself.

How do you feel in this picture? Are you feeling brave? Scared? Happy? Sad? Kind? Mad? Confused?

Draw a picture of your family.

How do you think each of them feel in this picture? Are they feeling brave? Scared? Happy? Sad? Kind? Mad? Confused?

Draw a picture of your friends.

How do you think each of them feel in this picture? Are they feeling brave? Scared? Happy? Sad? Kind? Mad? Confused?

Look at these pictures. Point to all the ones that show how you're feeling today.

sleepy

sad

happy

scared

hungry

bored

mad

in love

surprised

sick

confused

tired

Draw a picture of where you feel the safest. Are you snuggled under the covers in your own bed with your favorite toy? Are you in the kitchen eating your favorite food? Are you at school with your friends? Or are you someplace else? While you're drawing, ask yourself what makes you feel safe there.

Now keep this picture in your mind. So, if something happens to scare you, you can imagine your 'safe place' and it will make you feel better.

WHAT CAN YOU DO TO STAY SAFE?

Nature protects all of its creatures by giving each one a special gift to help them stay safe. Birds can fly away from danger. Bees can sting. Deer have horns. Kangaroos hop away. Skunks squirt out a very smelly spray when danger approaches them. Elephants stick together in herds. The opossum plays dead to fool its hunters.

Nature protects you, too, by giving you courage, strength and a brain to understand what you need to do to stay safe.

Here are 10 things you can do to stay safe from a terrorist:

1. Make your body strong and fit, so that you can run away, in case there's ever a terrorist attack near you. You can do this by eating healthy food, like fruit, vegetables, meat, and fish - not junk food, and drinking healthy beverages like juice, milk and water. You can make your body extra strong by taking vitamins.

2. Make your mind strong, too, so that you can think clearly in case of an emergency. You can do this by getting a good night's sleep every night for at least 8 hours. To have sweet dreams (and no nightmares), you need to do something relaxing before you go to bed – like take a warm bath or shower, read a bedtime story, have milk and a cookie, or talk to your mom, dad or a friend, especially if there is something bothering you. People who care about you can always make you feel better.

3. Exercise is very important for your body and your mind, too. Sitting in front of a computer or TV set all day, or lying on your bed texting with your friends, will make you lazy and sluggish. You need to have at least 30 minutes to an hour of exercise every day in order to stay fit and ready for action. This could be at school in P.E. class, or playing sports with your friends, or walking the dog around your neighborhood.

4. Pay attention in school and do your homework every day, so that you can learn a lot and go on to work at a job that will help keep America strong. We need smart people to build new things, and think out of the box. For example, we need doctors, lawyers, teachers, scientists, inventors, nurses, firefighters, police officers, paramedics, politicians, and people to work for the Federal Bureau of Investigation and for Homeland Security to keep America safe. Other jobs are very important, too.

5. Do not watch anything violent on TV, movies or other entertainment. Did you know that when a kid (or even an adult) watches a lot of violence – like where people are being shot, or hurt in other ways – it can make them want to copy what they watch and hurt other people, too? Most bullies watch a lot of violence that pushes them to be mean to other kids. Instead, watch stories with a more positive message, like saving animals, or comedies that make you laugh, or documentaries that teach you something about the world. These will make you feel so much better.

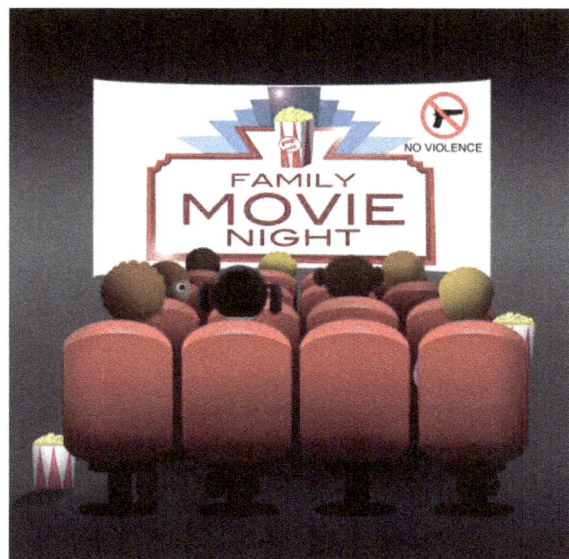

6. Spreading love is the best way to stop terrorism. You can do this in many ways every day. Tell your family that you love them and give them a hug. Tell your friends and other people you care about that you are happy that they are in your life. And do at least one act of kindness for someone you know, or even a stranger. You can help your mom with the dishes or help your friend with his homework. You can give up your seat on the bus to an elderly lady or give your allowance to a homeless veteran carrying a cup.

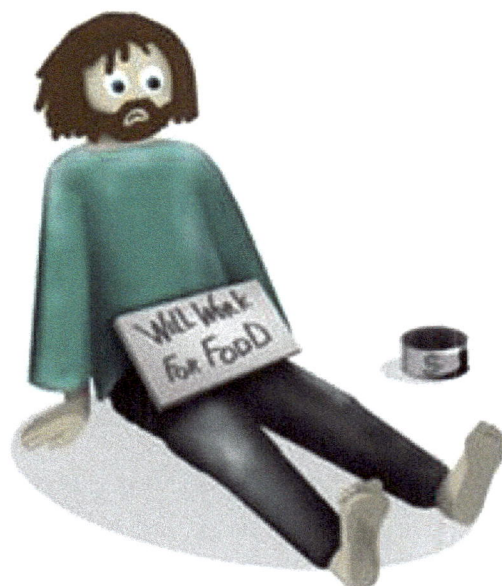

7. Kids can spot terrorists, too. You may have seen signs that read, "If you see something, say something!" This is asking us to report anything that seems suspicious – like someone purposely leaving a package with wires sticking out of it on a busy street, or a stranger at the airport asking a passenger to take something with him on the plane, or someone who keeps talking about how he hates this country. If you see something that seems suspicious, tell the closest adult, whether that's your parent, a teacher, a police officer, or any other adult nearby. You can help protect your country from terrorists by being a good detective.

8. There is a long word called "xenophobia." It means fear of strangers. Although you should report things or people who seem suspicious, it doesn't mean that you should suspect everyone who doesn't look like you, or who comes from a different country, or has a different religion than your family believes in. It's especially important to remember that not all Muslims are terrorists.

I'm a Muslim and I'm not a terrorist.

Most Muslims want peace, just like we do. And some terrorists – like the ones who were born in America – may not even be Muslims. They are just traitors. So, you should encourage your friends to get to know people and give them a chance to show you who they really are before assuming bad things about them.

9. Most importantly, don't let your fears about terrorists stop you from having fun and doing the usual things that you and your family like to do. Don't hide under the covers. Go out, have fun. Carry something with you – like a photo of your family and your pets - to remind you how much you are loved. Be thankful for the freedom and opportunities that the United States of America gives you. The Declaration of Independence promises "Life, Liberty and the pursuit of Happiness." Terrorists will never take this away from us!

10. Make a safety plan with your family so you know what to do in case of any scary situation – like a terrorist attack. You will probably be with some grownup – like your mother, father, other family member, teacher, babysitter, or friend's parent – if a terrorist attack occurs. They will tell you what to do to stay safe.

You can also call or text these people for help:

Mommy	Daddy	Sister/Brother	Other Family/Friend
---------------------	---------------------	---------------------	---------------------

Emergency Operator for police, firefighters, ambulance: 911

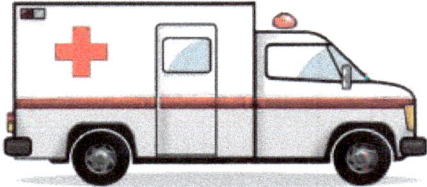

Addresses of places you plan to meet at:

Home	Parent's Work	School	Friend's House
_____	_____	_____	_____
_____	_____	_____	_____
_____	_____	_____	_____

Write down any other instructions that your family wants you to follow as part of your safety plan:

Now you know a lot about terrorism and terrorists, and what you can do to stay safe. If you have any more questions, ask your parents, teachers or other grownups, who have read this book with you. Always be sure to tell the people who care about you how you are feeling, so they can help you feel better. And remember, the best way to stop terrorism is to spread love, not fear.

"You have plenty of courage, I am sure," answered Oz. "All you need is confidence in yourself. There is no living thing that is not afraid when it faces danger. The true courage is in facing danger when you are afraid, and that kind of courage you have in plenty."

- L. Frank Baum, The Wonderful Wizard of Oz

About The Author

Carole Lieberman, M.D., M.P.H., internationally renowned as 'The Terrorist Therapist', is a Board Certified Beverly Hills psychiatrist. Since 9/11, Dr. Carole has been helping families overcome their fears of the ultimate monster under the bed... terrorism.

Her book, *Coping with Terrorism: Dreams Interrupted*, was published in London as the anniversary edition of 7/7, their most notable attack. Dr. Carole is a three-time Emmy-honored TV personality on top shows, radio talk show host, and best-selling author. Her Shrink-on-Board relaxation program calms fears in-flight and on the ground. Dr. Carole was Chief Resident in psychiatry at NYU-Bellevue and has served for decades on the Clinical Faculty of UCLA's Neuropsychiatric Institute.

For more information please visit us at:
www.terrorism4kids.com

About The Illustrator

Stephanie Conti, a native of Paris, received her degree in Visual Communications after completing her graduate studies. She has worked in Paris, London and Los Angeles as a graphic designer and model maker for advertising, TV shows and theater sets. As a sculptor, she's done several commissioned works, exhibited in art shows and organized art workshops for kids.